SCHUBERT

Overleaf: Portrait of Schubert by
Otto Nowak

Joseph Wechsberg

SCHUBERT

His Life   His Work

His Time

RIZZOLI
NEW YORK

First published in the United States of America in
1977 by:

Rizzoli INTERNATIONAL PUBLICATIONS, INC.
712 Fifth Avenue/New York 10019

Library of Congress Catalog Card Number: 77–77677
ISBN: 0–8478–0122–5

Printed in Great Britain

Contents

Foreword

Schubert's biographers often apologize for writing yet another book on him since so much has already been published. This foreword is not an apology but a belated declaration of love. It took me a long time to get close to the genius of Franz Schubert. A great many people are still badly mistaken about him. Perhaps more than any other immortal composer, Schubert has been affected by the evolution of time: it took almost a hundred years for his greatness to be discovered.

No one has found out anything new of basic importance about Franz Schubert since Professor Otto Erich Deutsch devoted his life to Schubert – the man, the musician, the 'hero of human culture', as Deutsch calls him. Like many other Schubert biographers, I have derived knowledge and inspiration from Otto Erich Deutsch's life work. Other experts are named when I refer to them. I have not tried to list all Schubert's works and I do not attempt musical analysis with notes and excerpts. That has been done before, and does not always help to make Schubert understood. Instead I write about the man and the artist, about his time and his Vienna, and that part of his work that is close to my heart – in particular his chamber and instrumental music, much of which I have played as a violinist.

Only a few years have passed since the latest books on Schubert were published, yet some are already outdated. The powerful influence of Franz Schubert moves on. I look at him as we feel about him today, with love and devotion, one hundred and fifty years after he died, mourned by his friends, an unrecognized genius.

Legend and Truth

Schubert is the best-loved and most misunderstood among the great composers. He is often portrayed as the happy-go-lucky bohemian, the composer of Merry Old Vienna, drinking and revelling in suburban wine gardens, a jolly companion with men but rather shy with the girls, dashing off a little music whenever he felt 'inspired'. This Schubert, the unreal one, became commercially valuable, the hero of operettas and cheap films. His catchy melodies were exploited by unscrupulous people who made more money out of him in a month than Schubert earned in his whole life.

This image of Schubert, the cosy Biedermeier character, still exists, and the operetta fairytales are the consequence of what Schubert's friends wrote about him. Long after he had died in 1828 the friends who had loved him and helped him while he was alive began reminiscing about him. They were old then and glorified the past, and they had nostalgic fantasies about 'Schwammerl' ('little mushroom') as they had nicknamed him. They had not really understood Schubert while he was alive and they did not try to understand him when he was dead. Consequently it has become difficult to see the genuine Schubert through the sentimental haze, the popular distortions. In 1857 his friend, the playwright Eduard von Bauernfeld, said that Schubert's life had so few conceivable biographical features that he could imagine 'only a sort of poetic description'. And in 1897 Max Friedländer, author of a valuable study on the German *Lied* in the eighteenth century and a noted Schubert scholar, said, 'There isn't enough material for a biography.'

Clichés are convenient for posterity. Bach remains 'the Thomas cantor, too learned and too dry'; Haydn, a true giant, was known as 'Papa Haydn', a silly label; for many people Mozart, the incredible miracle, is still a rococo figure, the *Wunderkind* whose picture appears on the chocolates named after him; Beethoven is 'The Titan', forever running through rain and storm; Verdi is shown as the mild-mannered old gentleman with his black felt hat. One could go on and on. But while almost all of them have at last been

An illustration for 'La Truite' by P. Sorrien.

LA TRUITE

PAR

FRANÇOIS SCHUBERT.
Prix: 3ᶠ.

recognized, Schubert remains widely misunderstood by the world at large after all these years. Even in his home town his greatness is not yet fully appreciated. Writing on 2 June 1976 in Vienna's *Die Presse* about *Schubert, As He Really Is*, Franz Endler discussed Schubert, 'the still misunderstood and posthumously disgraced musician'.

John Reed, the English musicologist, calls Schubert 'in modern times the most striking case of genius unrecognized, and in some cases the most puzzling'. Even musicians do not always understand him. During Schubert's short life – only a little more than thirty-one years – a very small part of his work was published. A few of his songs were sung after his death but no one in Vienna was interested in 'the rich treasure', as Grillparzer said, that Schubert had left. When Robert Schumann came to Vienna ten years after Schubert's death he found at the home of Schubert's brother Ferdinand piles of manuscripts no one had bothered to look at. In December 1839 Schumann wrote to Clara Wieck:

Clara, I was in a state of bliss today. At the rehearsal a symphony by Franz Schubert was played. If only you had been there! It is not possible to describe it to you: all the instruments are human voices. It is gifted beyond measure, this instrumentation, Beethoven notwithstanding, and this length, the heavenly length, like a novel in four volumes, longer than the Ninth Symphony. I was completely happy and wished for nothing but that you might be my wife, and that I, too, could write such symphonies.

And to his friend Ernst Adolf Becker in Freiburg, Schumann wrote the same day, 'Schubert's symphony is the greatest instrumental music that has been written since Beethoven, not excepting even Spohr and Mendelssohn'. Schumann was referring to the Great C major Symphony.

Few of Schubert's close friends were musicians. Instinctively he turned towards men of letters; he loved poetry. Among professional musicians Franz Lachner became close to Schubert in 1826, two years before the composer's death. Lachner was second *Kapellmeister* at Vienna's Kärntnertor-Theater and performed some of Schubert's music. Lachner later wrote chamber music and *Lieder* showing the influence of Schubert. But in 1884, when Lachner was in his eighties, he told Max Friedländer; 'Too bad that Schubert hadn't learned as much as I did, otherwise he would have become a master, for he was extraordinarily talented'. Lachner, speaking fifty-six years after Schubert's death, had obviously learned little himself. And Benedikt Randhartinger, a schoolmate of Schubert's who later became a composer and conductor, said, 'I regret that (Schubert) to the end of his life was a sort of dilettante.'

Beethoven, according to Anton Schindler, his first biographer, on his deathbed read some of Schubert's songs and said, 'Truly he has the divine spark.' The story may be true though Schindler is not always reliable. It would not have been the first time that genius recognized genius. On 12 February 1785 Leopold Mozart and Joseph Haydn were guests in Mozart's house in Vienna, and three new string quartets were played (K. 458, 464, 465) which Mozart had dedicated to Haydn. Then, as we know from one of Leopold Mozart's letters, Haydn turned to him and said: 'Before God and as an honest man I tell you that your son is the greatest composer known to me either in person or by name. He has taste and, what is more, the most profound knowledge of composition.' Haydn was then fifty-three, the most famous musician in Europe. Two years later he was one of the very few people in Vienna who understood the greatness of Mozart's ('this unique Mozart') *Don Giovanni*. Beethoven may have divined the genius of Schubert, who was often inspired and awed by him.

Schubert has been called 'the classicist of romanticism' and 'the romantic of classicism'. Indeed he lived and created at an epoch when two great eras of music converged into each other. There are no clear borderlines. Schubert's boundless prodigality reminds us of the unfathomable mystery of Mozart, although he remains close to Beethoven. Alone, he dared extend the faraway frontiers of Beethoven's creations. In his late masterpieces Schubert had visions of a new, post-Beethoven music. But as a composer Schubert always remained himself, though he had to live with the presence of Beethoven. In 1822 Schubert wrote what is known as his *Unfinished* Symphony. 'His greatness becomes fearful if we realize that this wonder of a symphony was written ... in the immediate vicinity of Beethoven's Ninth Symphony,' writes Paul Henry Lang. Yet the *Unfinished* Symphony remains the expression of Schubert's personal genius. Only he could have written it.

Schindler writes about Schubert's 'unhappy experience in 1822, when he presented to the Master (Beethoven) a copy of his *Variations for Four Hands* which he had dedicated to him'. The Vatiations Op. 10, written in 1818, are dedicated to Beethoven 'by his devoted admirer Franz Schubert'. According to Schindler:

The shy and speechless young composer contributed to his own embarrassment, in spite of the fact that he was introduced by Diabelli [the music publisher] who interpreted for him his feelings for the great man ... Schubert completely lost control of himself ... He rushed out of the house and bitterly reproached himself. He could never again summon up the courage to present himself before the great man.

A good story, but many biographers discount it as pure fiction. Schubert often met Beethoven in the street – Vienna was not a large city. But he never had the nerve to speak to his idol. He and Grillparzer walked behind the coffin at Beethoven's funeral.

Franz Schuppanzigh, one of Vienna's best violinists at the time of Beethoven, whose quartet gave the first performances of Beethoven's greatest string quartets, once played (according to Lachner) Schubert's String Quartet in D minor, *Der Tod und das Mädchen*, in Lachner's apartment. Much, much later Lachner remembered:

The quartet which now delights everybody and is counted among the greatest creations of its kind, by no means met with undivided approval. The first violin (Schuppanzigh) who on account of his great age was admittedly not equal to such a task,
declared to the composer, after playing it through, 'My dear fellow, this is no good,
leave it alone, and stick to your songs!' Whereupon Schubert silently packed up
the sheets of music and shut them away in his desk forever – a self denial and modesty
that one would look for in vain in many a present-day composer.

Again, we do not know whether we can trust Lachner's memory. According
to O.E. Deutsch the D minor Quartet, written late in 1825 and early in
1826, was first performed in the home of the noted tenor Josef Barth. The
quartet was posthumously published in 1831 and the manuscript is now lost.
We also know that towards the end of Schubert's life Schuppanzigh played
some of his chamber music and liked it. He may have changed his mind.

A 'Schubertiade'
painted by Julius
Schmid.

The Wienerwald, or Vienna Woods.

In 1827 the English musician Edward Holmes, a friend of the poet John Keats and a biographer of Mozart, wrote about Vienna's musical life of the time but failed to mention Schubert. Three years later the Belgian musicologist Fétis published *Curiosités Historiques de la Musique*. No word about Schubert. Heinrich Kreissle von Hellborn who wrote the first important Schubert biography in 1865 calls the beautiful, often mysterious *Trout* Quintet 'melodious and tame'. Joseph Joachim, the close friend of Brahms, complained about the 'shapelessness' of Schubert's String Quintet, one of his greatest works. Richard Wagner called Schubert a 'third-rate talent' and failed to understand what Franz Liszt saw in Schubert's 'philistine sonatas'. Liszt proved Schubert's greatness with his piano transcriptions of some Schubert *Lieder*. Though Liszt could not transcribe the text of the poems, he created small symphonic poems. Schubert's songs are the musical distillation of the poems he used. Schubert gave a new dimension even to some of Goethe's great poems. But the *Dichterfürst* arrogantly ignored Schubert, which has confused generations of Goethe and Schubert scholars. Perhaps Goethe sensed that Schubert was a genius who might even improve his poems, if that was humanly possible. 'Only through Schubert's music, Goethe's poems would be known to millions of people,' wrote Richard Capell in *Schubert's Songs*. Only an Englishman would dare make such a statement.

16

The list of the people who failed to understand Schubert is long and distinguished. Romain Rolland, Sir Hubert Parry, Vincent d'Indy who criticized Schubert's 'inadequate writing technique', and many others. Schubert was not infallible. He wrote masterpieces – we are concerned mainly with these – and he also wrote some mediocre music, though rarely bad. But the 'divine spark' was often there though most people did not notice it. When George Bernard Shaw, then a noted music critic, heard Schubert's Great C major Symphony in 1892 at London's Crystal Palace he concluded that 'the lamentable truth (is) that a more exasperatingly brainless composition was never put on paper'. That might go under Famous Early Words. But the following year Shaw wrote about a symphony by Hermann Goetz, now mercifully forgotten, 'Goetz had the charm of Schubert without his brainlessness.' Shaw made similar statements about Brahms and Verdi. But when his *Collected Music Reviews* were published in 1932 he had the good sense to exclude his youthful errors.

As late as 1962 the London Magazine *Music and Letters* published an article *Tales from the Vienna Backwoods* in which the author called *Heidenröslein* and *Die Post* 'as cheap as the words' and *Das Wandern ist des Müllers Lust*, which has become a folk song, 'the incarnation of commonplace'. Why should we be surprised that the Vienna Philharmonic Orchestra, in 1895, 'regretfully' turned down a request for a ticket from Schubert's youngest brother Andreas who had been born in 1823, five years before Franz died. Poor Andreas wanted to hear his famous brother's Great C major Symphony. Vienna's venerable *Gesellschaft der Musikfreunde*, founded in 1812, has a long list of honorary members, from Beethoven, Berlioz, Brahms, Bruckner to Schumann, Richard Strauss, Verdi, Wagner. Schubert is not among them. He is only a member of the *Repräsentantenkörper*, whatever that means. It is now explained that he was 'too young' to be elected. Other not-so-young non-members are Mahler and Schönberg.

Can so many people be wrong? Maybe not. Schubert is often erratic and diffuse. As a composer of instrumental music he sometimes strives in vain for 'classical' clarity. He was a romantic at heart and was at his best when he wrote songs. He was almost always original, sometimes uninhibited, often creating another version of the same poem when he was not satisfied with the first. His lyrical piano pieces, the impromptus and dances, are truly musical moments of great beauty, sudden inspirations of a lyrical poet. He never wrote closely-knit piano sonatas or classically cool string quartets. He would inject ideas from songs and lyrical moods, breaking up the strict sonata form, which caused his critics to call his work 'shapeless'. There are bewitching moments in his instrumental music but critics said 'the movements do not hold together'.

Unlike Beethoven and many other composers Schubert almost never made preliminary sketches. He did the preliminary work in his head. Some writers put down the final version of what they want to say; they do not re-write, having previously done the revisions in their mind. This was the way Schubert worked. He refused to revise anything he did not like. He would start all over again and try a second or third version. His friend Spaun wrote, 'Schubert would never polish his compositions, so that tedious passages or inaccuracies occur here and there.' It was not always the last versions of his songs that were published, and this created confusion. In accordance with contemporary practice Schubert did not indicate every detail in his scores. But he was careful about the dynamic nuances, writing in *crescendo* and *diminuendo*, which is important for the singing voice.

The critics also reproved him for leaving some works unfinished. But in Vienna the unfinished work of art has always been an accepted art form. St Stephen's Cathedral, the city's symbol, is unfinished. Mozart, Beethoven, Schubert, Bruckner, Mahler, Grillparzer, Musil and many others left unfinished masterpieces. Schubert's *Unfinished* Symphony, however, is neither unfinished nor his last. He wrote two, possibly three, more symphonies afterwards. Of the Symphony in E minor/E major only the slow introduction and 110 bars of the first movement survive. The Great C major Symphony exists in its entirety. And the mysterious, sometimes mentioned, *Gmunden-Gastein* Symphony remains a genuine enigma.

According to O.E. Deutsch's *Thematic Catalogue of Schubert's Works in Chronological Order* Schubert left 12 symphonies, 10 overtures, 3 pieces for violin and orchestra, 3 string quintets, 22 string quartets, 2 string trios, 22 sonatas for piano, 40 fantasies, impromptus and similar pieces, 452 dances for piano, 634 songs (and some 100 variations), and many other works. Deutsch accounts for a total of 1515 works but the list is not definitive. Some works are lost, and some are still being discovered, though rarely. A great many of Schubert's original manuscripts are lost, and this does not facilitate the work of his editors. Most of his autographs are at the Stadtbibliothek (City Library) of Vienna, and there are many at the Musikverein.

It is sometimes hard to believe that Schubert in his short life had so many musical ideas, but the evidence is there. Obviously not everything he wrote was perfect but a creative artist should be judged after his best work, and Schubert's best is very great. Hans Gal writes, 'For Schubert's instrumental style, as for his songs, the negative rule applies, that his music must never become subservient to the metronome.' That is true. Some elements in Schubert's music shock the unrestricted theorist. Schubert is always singing – with his voice, on the piano, in his chamber music, in his orchestral works. Some

people feel there is no true form, no guiding hand, no strict discipline. But the discipline becomes apparent in his late works when he no longer had the innocence of youth, though he always remained young at heart.

The 'Römische Kaiser' coffeehouse in Vienna.

In 1885 Brahms advised Richard Strauss, then a young musician, to study Schubert's dances for their melodic structure. 'Try to write simple, eight-bar melodies,' he said. And, 'To construct the melodic shape is a question of talent. But here we are also concerned with one of the most difficult technical problems . . . A melody that seems to have been born in a short moment is almost always the result of hard work.' Mozart and Schubert were masters of such melodies and the 'lightness' is proof of their genius. Sixty years later Strauss wrote a thirty-seven-bar reminiscence of Franz Schubert in his sketch book – he was then working on *Metamorphosen* – and wrote, 'Lucky Schubert who could compose what he wanted, whatever his genius made him do.' Quite an admission for Richard Strauss, never outstanding for modesty.

19

Dietrich Fischer-Dieskau, one of the best Schubert singers, makes an important point: 'Schubert writes as he thinks, as he feels, as he speaks ... That may be called natural style. We don't claim that a natural style is proof of a great composer. But the musician who writes a natural style is one of the wonders of music.'

opposite The
Dreimäderlhaus.

People who love Schubert are happy with his sudden melodious inventions and lyrical moments. Whenever my friends and I play his magnificent A minor Quartet Op. 29, the distilled essence of his genius, we always discover more hidden treasures in this work, which contains the whole range of Schubert's musical imagination. The melancholy beauty of the first movement, the heavenly simplicity of the Andante, the Minuet that has been called 'a stroke of genius', the brilliant Finale. Is it a 'formless' work, as some critics have claimed? Perhaps, for those who believe in what Goethe called 'grey theory'. For us, who cherish 'life's golden tree', the A minor Quartet remains the true expression of Schubert's musicianship.

Yet we must avoid the misconception of many learned experts that the 'profound' Schubert – who wrote the great quartets, the C major Quintet, the Great C major Symphony, the *Winterreise* cycle – is the one and only Schubert. That is nonsense. We accept Schubert in his 'profound' and his light moments, in his Beethoven-like aspirations and in his carefree moods when he wrote the dances and melodies in *Rosamunde*, even the mishmash of tunes that form the score of the *Dreimäderlhaus*. All this is Schubert. If you love a composer you do not accept just part of his work and reject the rest. Genius has many facets, and Schubert's is no exception. He wrote great music and he wrote popular music. But whatever he wrote it was always Schubert.

His life offers some clues but he can be really understood only through his music – a laborious task, since there is so much of it. Most discoveries have already been made but to appreciate the very greatness of Schubert you must try to make your own discoveries. It may be a *Lied*, a quartet movement, part of a symphony, a piano composition. Probably it will be a sudden, lovely melody – so sweet and simple that you wonder: 'Why didn't I think of it myself?'

Schubert's Vienna

Seventeen days before Schubert was born the Austrian troops were defeated at Arcole and Rivoli, on 14 January 1797. On 12 February Joseph Haydn's new national anthem *Gott erhalte Franz den Kaiser*, that had been 'ordered' a few months earlier, was first sung in all Austrian theatres. It might have created less enthusiasm had the people known that on the same day the troops of Napoleon Bonaparte had overrun the Austrian-dominated fortress of Mantua in Italy. Haydn's beautiful anthem failed to outlive the Habsburgs in Austria. Since 1918 it has been considered taboo there, a 'monarchist' melody, though it gloriously survives in the *poco adagio* movement of Haydn's Kaiser-Quartet Op. 76, No. 3. It is now the national anthem of the Federal Republic of Germany where it has no damnable monarchist associations. The present Austrian anthem, by Mozart, is no match for Haydn's immortal melody.

On 14 April when Schubert was seventy-six days old, Vienna's Landsturm troops marched through Nussdorferstrasse (as it is now known) past the house where Franz Schubert had been born. A brass band preceded the soldiers. Their rendition of the new Haydn anthem may have been the baby's first musical impression. Later that year, the Habsburgs were forced to sign the peace treaty of Campo Formio, losing Lorraine and their Burgundian possessions, and also Lombardy. After Napoleon defeated the Austrians at Marengo, the Habsburgs lost Tuscany, which was signed over in the peace treaty of Lunéville.

In 1805 Napoleon reached Vienna. The premiere of Beethoven's *Fidelio* at the Theater an der Wien took place before an audience of French officers; the opera was a failure. After the peace treaty of Pressburg the Habsburgs lost Venetia and had to cede the old dominion of Tyrol to Napoleon's ally, the Elector of Bavaria. This disaster was followed by the war of 1809 that brought the Austrian troops under Archduke Karl their only victory, at Aspern. But then the Emperor Napoleon I defeated the Austrians at Wagram and forced the Habsburgs to sign the treaty of Schönbrunn. They lost

opposite above Vienna from the Bastions.

opposite below Napoleon's bivouac at Austerlitz in 1805.

25

Carinthia, Carniola, Friuli, Dalmatia and Galicia. The final bitter touch for Emperor Franz was the marriage of Napoleon, who had divorced Josephine de Beauharnais, to Princess Marie-Louise, the Emperor's sixteen-year-old daughter. The upstart from Corsica had become the son-in-law of the Head of the House of Habsburg. Franz Schubert was twelve years old.

Earlier in 1804 the Kaiser, who had the title of Franz II, Holy Roman Emperor, had assumed the more modest, hereditary crown of the Emperor of Austria and as such called himself Franz I. Two years later he was forced by Napoleon to decree that the Holy Roman Empire had ceased to exist. By 1810 Europe had changed. Napoleon's nominees were sitting on ancient and new thrones all over the continent. Eventually the nightmare ended after twenty-three years of fighting. Napoleon was on St Helena, safely out of the way. In 1815 the Congress of Vienna tried to hammer out a new order for Europe which more or less lasted ninety-nine years – until the outbreak of the First World War in 1914.

The Congress of Vienna, 1814–1815.

Schubert's entire childhood, from 1797 to 1808 when he was eleven and admitted to the Court Chapel, was overshadowed by the war years. Twice, once when he was eight and later when he was twelve years old, Vienna was occupied by the French. In 1815, while many Viennese were fascinated by the antics of the Congress, Schubert was a prolific composer. On 19 August of that year he wrote five *Lieder*, among them the immortal *Heiden-röslein* that will probably survive the memories of the Congress of Vienna. On 25 August he wrote six more and on 15 October he wrote eight songs. Some people conclude that he was a sloppy worker. The truth is that he was a genius. From Moritz von Schwind, one of Schubert's best friends and later a distinguished painter, we know that Schubert sometimes had no manuscript paper when he was in the mood to compose. Using pen and ruler Schwind would quickly transform sketching paper into three-stave music paper. He would give Schubert an old anthology of poems. Eduard Hanslick, the critic, reported in 1863: 'Schubert had hardly read them before his pen

'The Outing' by Moritz von Schwind.

27

A view of the Kohlmarkt in Vienna enamelled onto a glass in 'Biedermeier' style.

opposite above St Stephen's Cathedral in Vienna; watercolour by R. Alt.

opposite below A tavern scene painted by Neder.

overleaf A view of Vienna with the bastions in the mid-19th century.

was gliding merrily over the paper ... Schwind maintains to this day that those music lines were not the least valuable he ever drew.' If the story is true, it might add to the mystery of creative genius.

After 1815, when people settled down trying to forget the horrors of the past, until 1848, when they rose against their rulers and several waves of revolutions shook Europe, Vienna went through that strange era known as the Biedermeier and the *Vormärz* (pre-March). This period is remembered, fondly or sarcastically, as *Alt Wien* (Old Vienna); the era of cosiness and *Gemütlichkeit* (leave me alone please), today still practised under the motto Mei Ruh' will i ham (I want to have my peace), of small bourgeois homes and rose gardens, people spending their afternoon at the Heuriger inn, drinking the young wine, singing, enjoying the small pleasures of life. It is a sentimental, beguiling legend, and Schubert is part of it. But it is not strictly true.

The era became known as Biedermeier only around 1850, when it was all over. The German satirical weekly *Fliegende Blätter* published *Biedermayers Liederlust*, ironical poems by a German writer L. Eichrodt. The fictitious author of the poems was a Swabian schoolteacher, Gottlieb Biedermayer, whose style of life was later derided. Somehow the name Biedermeier remained as the symbol of an era that had actually existed. In the small towns of the Wienerwald foothills there are still Biedermeier houses, cosy and lovely to look at – though perhaps not so pleasant to live in – where time seems to have stopped for a hundred and fifty years. 'If one speaks of Old Vienna, one thinks of the times of Schubert and Raimund, of the Emperor Franz and Metternich,' wrote Alois Trost the Viennese writer. Well, not always.

It took a long time to destroy the legend of Schubert being a symbol of the Biedermeier era. He did live at that time and in a superficial way he displays some of its characteristics. But his music – and the music does not lie – proves that he was anything but a Biedermeier character. Thirty-five years after the event, Moritz von Schwind painted a watercolour dripping with nostalgia. It shows Franz Schubert and two friends sitting in a Grinzing Heuriger garden, at a small table with three glasses and a flagon of young wine. The church of Grinzing is in the rear and there are the soft contours of Kahlenberg and Leopoldsberg. Schubert's face is round and his hair is unkempt. One friend is the conductor Franz Lachner, the other is the playwright Eduard von Bauernfeld, who liked good fun but was actually a rebel against the tough, reactionary régime of Metternich and his chief of police, Count Joseph von Sedlnitzky. Schwind's watercolour is both true and a fairytale. But nowhere are reality and legend blended so closely as in Vienna.

The Biedermeier, that bourgeois idyl, was also the era of police informers and crowded prisons. The police spied on many citizens and would open all letters of suspect persons. If telephones had already existed they would have tapped them. The definition of Austria as 'absolutism, mitigated by slovenliness' dates from a later time but applies to the Biedermeier. The secret police were *schlampig* but could be very unpleasant. One morning in 1820 Schubert's school friend Johann Chrysostomus Senn was arrested for 'having uttered rebellious thoughts' against Count Sedlnitzky. Senn and some friends, among them Schubert, had held an allegedly 'libertarian' meeting at an inn that actually might have been quite innocuous. Schubert, according to O.E. Deutsch, escaped with a black eye, and was released after a few hours. Senn remained in prison for fourteen months, suspected of activities that were never proved, and was sent into 'exile' in far away Tyrol. He never forgot his humiliation and died as an angry, bitter eccentric. So much for *Gemütlichkeit*. Schubert knew well what was happening but continued to set to music some poems of Senn that he liked.

Most of Schubert's friends, the *Schubertianer*, played the role of cheerful middle class people who would never think of plotting against authority; but they were pretending. Ferdinand Raimund, the playwright and not a Schubertian, escaped into a world of fairytales and innuendo. Franz Grillparzer, Austria's greatest poet, suffered 'a typical Austrian fate', doing everything wrong. He knew Schubert but was not a member of the composer's inner circle. Only in his posthumously published writings did Grillparzer reveal how much he had suffered under censorship and restrictions. Austria's great writers of the epoch often had spells of melancholy, or morbid hypochondria. They remained misunderstood and isolated and were depressed by their isolation. Raimund and Adalbert Stifter committed suicide; Nikolaus Lenau's depression ended in madness; Johann Nestroy was often despondent; and Grillparzer became a bitter misanthrope.

Schubert escaped the 'typical Austrian fate'. He and his friends were hiding in a fairytale world of wine, women and songs. They knew that the dream was better than the harsh reality. An entry in Schubert's (lost) diary of 1824 speaks of onesidedness 'which makes so many wretches think that only what *they* are doing is best while everything else is of no account. *One* beauty should inspire a man throughout his whole life, it is true; but the splendour of that inspiration should illuminate everything else.' Schubert was no early revolutionary, but neither was he a fool who did not know what was going on around him.

Much was happening. Metternich and his henchman, Friedrich von Gentz, were not from Vienna. Metternich was the scion of an old Rhineland

opposite above Schubert's piano.

opposite below The decorated façade of a house in upper Austria.

Metternich by Thomas Lawrence.

family. Gentz had been born in Breslau, Silesia, in 1764. Both had ability and strong reactionary principles. They had nothing against the Viennese as long as the citizens behaved like true Biedermeier paragons. Both were obsessed by the student movements at the German universities.

'I feel certain that a whole generation of revolutionaries is bred (at the universities),' Metternich wrote to Gentz on 17 June 1819. 'The evil must be contained ... The greatest and therefore the most urgent evil today is the press.' Gentz later said that 'the security of our censorship has protected our monarchy from being invaded by this pestilential poison'. He was referring to critical political journalism. He praised the State that had remained, 'so calm and happy in the paternal care of a virtuous sovereign'. Neither he nor Metternich seemed to have heard of the existence of one Franz Schubert, *Compositeur*, in Vienna. If they had, they could not have cared less.

His Apostolic Majesty, 'The good Emperor Franz' as he remains known in Haydn's beautiful anthem, was not truly interested in music, as were his

A view of Nussdorf near Vienna, 1830.

predecessors, who had at least taken notice of Gluck and Mozart. Schubert contributed to the imperial mythos when he composed in January 1822 Johann Ludwig Ferdinand Deinhardtstein's four-verse hymn *Am Geburtstag des Kaisers*. Leopold Sonnleithner had arranged for the commission, and Schubert wrote the music even though his heart was not in it, and his melody never reaches Haydn's inspiring beauty.

Perhaps Schubert, no fool, had heard too much about Emperor Franz who remained 'his' emperor during his entire life. As a young man the Emperor had been shaken by the trauma of the French Revolution, and later he was humiliated by Napoleon. He evolved a clever technique of never making an instantaneous decision – 'letting things lie' – and after the bread riots of 1805 he kept a garrison in Vienna, just in case. According to *Bilder aus Oestreich aus den Jahren 1848–49*, by a German traveller:

... the emperor gave a masterly stage performance in public. By birth and disposition a foreigner, in the disagreeable sense of the word, he played 'the bogus Viennese'

The Leopoldstadt seen from Jüngling coffee-house.

35

throughout his life. The ordinary people of Vienna, of Austria and Styria, possess an indestructible fund of harmless sincerity, cheerfulness and good humour. The man in the street is charming. Franz, by nature a suspicious, crafty coldhearted and narrow-minded prince, without magnanimity, yet with a sharp eye for the weaknesses of the broad masses of the people; so cultured that he could express himself with diplomatic care and precision in both French and Italian – disguised his most carefully calculated thoughts in the simple Viennese dialect, and aped the homely simplicity of the people in gesture, expression and movement, so regularly and for so long that the mask eventually became his regular face. The emperor's example set the fashion ...

That was 'the good Emperor Franz' who once told a deputation of schoolmasters, 'I don't need scholars, I need obedient subjects.' He demanded the absolute submissiveness of his subjects although he played second violin in string quartets because he knew he could not have played first. And this was the man who helped to create the climate of Schubert's Biedermeier Vienna, and, indirectly, the mood of Schubert's friends. We know a great deal about them, owing to the life work of Professor Deutsch. In the preface to his monumental Schubert biography O. E. Deutsch writes:

This is a book of facts, the self-print of a life. It is different from other biographies: it doesn't select events and evidence that became known to the author. It doesn't bridge gaps and doesn't connect the material in a belletristic or scientific way. Instead it is ... an approximately complete collection of all facts and documents, and of the necessary explanations. These explanations are written in an objective manner. Thus this book attempts to be the natural monument of Schubert's life: heroic, as it becomes to a hero of human culture.

In 1820, when Schubert was twenty-three and at the height of his artistic imagination, the aristocrats who had been Beethoven's patrons – the Princes Lichnovsky, Lobkowitz, Rasumovsky, Galitzin – were no longer running Vienna's musical life. The new middle classes had taken over. They could not afford private orchestras or private string quartets but they loved house music and in 1812 had founded the Society of the Friends of Music. The Musikfreunde Society has survived improbable disasters in the past one hundred and fifty years, and is still in charge of the more conservative section of Vienna's musical life. Herbert von Karajan is its director for his lifetime. The Konzerthausgesellschaft represents the more progressive elements. They dare feature modern music and pop music. Vienna's musical traditions, going back to the days before Gluck and Haydn, were never interrupted. Musically, Vienna remains conservative.

When Schubert grew up and began to write music most of the musical gods were no longer around. Mozart had died in 1791, before Schubert was born, and Haydn died in 1809 when Schubert was twelve. Beethoven was

opposite above The old Burgtheater around 1810.

opposite below Old Grinzing near Vienna.

37

still there. Even Metternich's state police left him alone because they considered him 'harmless'. To his diary Schubert once confided, 'Who can still try to attempt anything after Beethoven?' He was deeply shocked by the death of Beethoven in 1827. It is possible that the shock contributed to his own end twenty months later. His last wish, to be buried near Beethoven, was fulfilled.

right A sketch of Schubert by Moritz von Schwind.

below A portrait of the artist Moritz von Schwind.

We know what Schubert looked like because some of his friends were gifted painters. Leopold Kupelwieser drew and painted Schubert. Wilhelm August Rieder left a famous watercolour, a lithography and several oil paintings. From Josef Teltscher we have a lithography and a coloured drawing. Schwind, seven years younger than Schubert, made several paintings of Schubert after the death of his friend. Josef Kriehuber's popular portrait was etched in 1846. Deutsch considers Rieder's watercolour the best portrait of Schubert. In 1825 Johann Passini made a copperplate engraving of it that was sold by Cappi & Co, the music publishers. Schubert was still alive and he was getting better known in Vienna.

All Schubert portraits show a short, undistinguished man with tousled hair, a high forehead, a round face and thick glasses, usually wearing a stiff high collar and a large butterfly tie. A cheerful man, wistful and lost in thought – a real Biedermeier type, one would say. 'So far as his body is concerned, one might imagine him as a fat lump,' Spaun wrote. 'But this is incorrect. Schubert had a solidly built, thick-set body but there was no question of his being fat.'

There is no trace of genius which we think we see in the face of Beethoven, none of the arrogance of Wagner, the dignity of Brahms. Schubert looks like a nice drinking companion, an amiable fellow rather than a lonely genius standing close to Haydn, Mozart, Beethoven. A Chinese proverb says that a picture tells more than a thousand words. Not in the case of Schubert. If one did not know that this was him, one would not look twice.

The Early Years

Franz Peter Schubert was born at half-past one, in the afternoon of 31 January 1797, in the sign of Aquarius like Mozart. The house *Zum Roten Krebsen* (At the Red Crab) was at No. 72, Himmelpfortgrund, in the Liechtental suburb of Vienna. It is now No. 54, Nussdorferstrasse, in the ninth district, and contains a Schubert Museum. Liechtental was founded by Johann Adam Prince Liechtenstein who built the nearby Rossau Garden Palais. The famous Liechtenstein Art Collections were kept there until 1940 when they were wisely removed to Vaduz in Liechtenstein.

Schubert's parents had fourteen children of whom five survived; Franz was the fourth. Between 1786 and 1801 his mother gave birth to twelve children in a tiny apartment, consisting of a small, primitive kitchen that is a narrow anteroom, and one medium-sized room, and there the family lived. It must have been rather crowded and quite a few children died but Franz survived and became immortal. When one stands in the kitchen where he was born it seems like a miracle.

The house with its simple two-storey façade was renovated after 1908 and re-opened in 1912. The present museum was started in 1953 under the control of Otto Erich Deutsch, who wanted to recreate the truth – at least as much of it as had become known. Originally there were sixteen 'apartments' on the ground floor and the upper floor; each 'apartment' consisted of a kitchen and living room and a small attic. When Schubert's father moved in there in 1786 he lived on the ground floor. Later he moved to the upper floor where Franz was born. The kitchen window opened into the courtyard and behind it was the small garden. The rear of the house consists of two wings. It would have been comfortable for the Schubert family if they had inhabited most of it, but they had to share it with fifteen other tenants. The interior of the house was later changed but its partition into tiny apartments can easily be recognized.

On the walls of the museum there are copies of Schubert portraits, Leopold Kupelwieser's Atzenbrugg watercolours and other pictures, and documents

opposite The courtyard of the house in which Schubert was born, in Liechtental.

43

opposite above The exterior of the house in which Schubert was born.

opposite below The church at Liechtental.

and manuscript pages, among them a sample from the *Unfinished* Symphony and *Der Lindenbaum* with Schubert's very neat handwriting. There is the piano that his father bought after Franz wrote his first Mass, in F major, and became famous in the suburb of Liechtental. And there is a beautiful chest of drawers which stood in the apartment of Schubert's older brother Ferdinand, where Franz died.

Schubert's father, Franz Theodor Florian Schubert, had moved from Moravia to Vienna. In 1786 he became schoolmaster in the Himmelpfortgrund. Eighteen months earlier he had married Maria Elizabeth Katharina Vietz (or Vitz), the daughter of a locksmith. She had worked in Vienna as a cook before her marriage and her family had come from Silesia to Vienna. Even then many Viennese came from elsewhere. Maria Elizabeth was a quiet woman who was loved by her children. When she died of typhoid fever – as Schubert did – Franz was fifteen years old. Ten years later, in 1822, Schubert wrote an 'allegorical story', *My Dream*. '... I was told of my mother's death. I rushed to see her; my father didn't hinder my entrance. I saw her lying. Tears streamed out of my eyes ... We followed her, mourning, and the bier disappeared ...' If *My Dream* is autobiographical (which we do not know) Schubert must have been deeply devoted to his mother.

One year after his wife's death, Schubert's father married Anna Kleyenböck, the daughter of a modest silk manufacturer. A mother was urgently needed for the children. She was twenty years younger than her husband, and fourteen years older than her stepson Franz. He was fond of her. She and the older Schubert later had five children of their own.

Schubert spent less than five years in the house where he was born. In 1801 the Schuberts moved into a larger house a short walk down the street – Säulengasse 3. A memorial tablet reminds pilgrims that Schubert once lived there and created many works, among them *Erlkönig*. (Now the house has become the Schubert Garage, specializing in Volkswagen repairs.) Schubert went from there to grammar school. He was the best pupil in his class, apparently a bright boy. Life in the family was dominated by loyalty to the House of Habsburg and by devotion to the Church. Schubert's father was later appointed Principal of a larger school in the Rossau district, and in 1826 was given the Freedom of the City 'for his useful services to education'. He was an orthodox believer in Fatherland and Clerus, which created problems between him and his sons. He died in 1830, eighteen months after the death of Franz Schubert. His widow survived him by almost thirty years.

Schubert's Vienna was not a large city. Around 1800 about 50,000 people lived in the Inner City and 170,000 in the suburbs. After the Napoleonic

wars the population grew. In 1824 there were 290,000 inhabitants in the city, among them 40,000 foreigners, many from Germany and Switzerland. Geographically the Inner City, with 50,000 people living in about 1200 houses in 127 streets, was surrounded by a U-shaped semicircle – the city walls (*Bastei*) and the moat (*Glacis*) that formed a fortified ring reaching towards the Danube Canal. After 1860 the ramparts facing the Danube Canal were razed and a wide boulevard was laid out, today's Kai. Other sections took longer to disappear but eventually the ramparts there were also destroyed, the moats and ditches were filled, and in 1865 the Ringstrasse was opened when Emperor Franz Joseph I and Empress Elizabeth drove along it for the first time. At last Vienna had its *via triumphalis*.

Beyond the *Glacis*, in Schubert's time, were the old *Vorstädte* (suburbs) which were surrounded by the *Linienwall*, another fortified half-circle leading towards the Danube. It dated from the Second Turkish Siege in 1683. Today this outer 'ring' is called the *Gürtel*. *Bastei* and *Glacis* had been there since the Middle Ages. Only the Leopoldstadt with Prater and Augarten, located between the Danube and the Danube Canal, were not fortified. The French invaders destroyed some fortifications in 1809 but they were rebuilt in 1816, after the Congress of Vienna. Twelve gates within the Inner City walls led into the thirty-four suburbs with 7000 houses.

Beyond the outer *Linienwall* were the rural *Vororte* – different from the urban *Vorstädte* – that reached into the foothills of the Wienerwald. These hills formed a third semicircle towards the Danube, with flat or hilly ground. The vineyards of the Heuriger taverns were there, the small Biedermeier houses, the sleepy streets and quiet squares. Beethoven loved the *Vororte*, especially Grinzing and Heiligenstadt. Schubert spent his childhood in the urban suburbs but later stayed often with friends in the Inner City. The wealthy people lived there; the twenty dukes, seventy counts and sixty barons who took a dim view of the lower aristocracy – *Landmänner, Edle von, Herren von* – many of them high-ranking officers, honoured civil servants, ennobled bankers, manufacturers, merchants whose wealth often surpassed their prestige. There were 2000 private carriages in the Inner City and 600 fiacres (horse-drawn coaches) for hire.

Himmelpfortgrund had 3000 inhabitants who lived in ninety houses in nine streets. Many people were well known; Father Schubert, the school-master, was respected in the neighbourhood. Franz Schubert's early life was surrounded by music. In Vienna around 1800 music was a way of life and a schoolmaster had to be a musician. Father Schubert taught Franz the rudiments of violin playing, and his oldest brother Ignaz gave him his first piano lessons. When the child appeared to be a musical prodigy the father asked

A house in
Wipplingerstrasse.

Michael Holzer, choirmaster of the Liechtental parish church, to teach
Franz singing, organ-playing and counterpoint. Schubert showed his gratitude when he dedicated his C major Mass to Holzer in 1816. According
to Schubert's favourite brother, Ferdinand, Holzer was often perplexed by
his bright pupil. 'Whenever I wanted to teach him anything, he already
knew it. I often stared at him in silent astonishment.'

Schubert's lifelong love affair with chamber music goes back to his early
days. The family had its own string quartet. Ignaz and Ferdinand played
the violin, the father played the cello, and Franz played the viola – a
favourite instrument with many composers, from Mozart and Beethoven to
Dvořák and Hindemith. Franz was the youngest member of the family quartet, and the strictest. When his father played a wrong note, which happened
often, Franz would interrupt and tell his father, respectfully but firmly, that

Schubert's brothers
Ignaz (*right*) and Carl
(*far right*).

below Schubert's sister
Thérèse in 1878.

something was not quite right. He composed his first string quartets in 1811 and 1812, both in D major and both now lost. He wrote three more in 1812, when he was fifteen, and they still show the influence of Haydn and Mozart. All his life Schubert played and wrote chamber music. We chamber musicians are grateful to him for some of the finest string quartets, *the* finest string quintet (with two cellos), the octet, and several works with piano.

In 1808 Schubert, then eleven, passed the strict examinations and was admitted as a chorister to the Imperial Court Chapel. A good singing voice and a certain knowledge of composition were obligatory. Dr Franz Innocenz Lang, head of the Stadtkonvikt which was the principal boarding school for commoners in Vienna as well as being the choir school, and Antonio Salieri, the Court Music Director who was much maligned for his opposition to Mozart, were among the members of the commission that listened to the examinations. (Seventy years earlier young Joseph Haydn had been a chorister at St Stephen's in Vienna.) Schubert received his secondary education at the Stadtkonvikt, founded in 1803, in the old university building next to the Jesuit church (which is still there). Schubert was often commended 'in general behaviour and studies'. He was especially good in singing, piano and the violin; he was able to read difficult pieces at sight. He learned a lot and made many friends and was quite popular at the Stadtkonvikt. Discipline was strict, food was scarce, and the boys were often hungry. On 24 November 1812, one year before leaving the Stadtkonvikt, Schubert wrote to his brother Ferdinand:

... I've come to the conclusion that life is pretty good though in some ways it could be better ... One could certainly do with a roll and a few apples, particularly when one has to wait eight and a half hours between a moderate sized midday meal and a wretched sort of supper ... The few groschen that Father gave me vanished into thin air in the first few days, so what am I going to do for the rest of the time? They who hope upon Thee shall not be put to shame. St Matthew 3:4. Too true! How would it be then if you were to let me have a few kreuzer each month? You wouldn't notice them and they would make me happy and contented in my cell.

A charming letter from a sixteen-year-old boy, proving Schubert's sense of humour. The alleged quotation is not in St Matthew's Gospel. Schubert made it all up.

Life at the Stadtkonvikt was no bed of roses but Schubert met some boys there who became friends for life. Among them was Joseph von Spaun. After Schubert's voice had broken he was permitted to stay on. Salieri personally taught Schubert counterpoint and Italian vocal writing. Schubert listened respectfully but he was already ahead of his teacher, and he was writing his own music which was not exactly Salieri's music. Salieri, Italian-trained,

A very early portrait of Schubert.

49

above Antonio Salieri, who was director of the Stadtkonvikt when Schubert was a student there.

below Joseph Lanner in the uniform of the Kapellmeisters.

made no effort to understand Schubert's harmonic, essentially German musical imagination. Salieri studied with his pupil the works of Gluck but he had no sympathy for Schubert's secret passion, the German *Lied*. Spaun remembers that 'the poems of Goethe, Schiller and others that inspired the young composer, remained for the Italian unusable ... He only read "barbaric words" that couldn't be set to music.' Spaun later remembered that Schubert had been much impressed by Mozart's G minor Symphony and Beethoven's Second, but Schubert's friends, in their reminiscences, do not agree on his 'favourite' composers. Anselm Hüttenbrenner, another friend, mentions Handel's *Messiah*, Mozart's *Don Giovanni* and the *Requiem*, and Beethoven's C minor Symphony. Benedikt Randhartinger, an early Stadtkonvikt friend, said, 'Schubert seldom expressed an unfavourable opinion about living artists. His ideal was Beethoven, all other composers mattered little to him.' And Spaun wrote much later, in 1858, 'After a performance of the *Figaro* Overture Schubert said, "That is the most beautiful overture in the whole world", but then added after some reflection, "I had almost forgotten *Die Zauberflöte*."' Probably all friends were right. Schubert loved good music and he had good taste. Among his early compositions dating from that time are some church music, two overtures and three symphonies.

The Stadtkonvikt's student orchestra had complete string sections, flutes, oboes, clarinets, bassoons, horns, trumpets and drums. Schubert played first violin and was later assistant conductor. His classmate Anton Holzapfel remembered that they performed the Haydn and Mozart symphonies, the first two Beethoven symphonies, and the *Coriolanus* and *Leonore* Overtures. But they did not play very well and had bad instruments. They loved the string quartets by Haydn and Mozart. It was a solid 'classical' education. In his *History of Concert Life in Vienna* Eduard Hanslick reports that 'in summer these performances by the pupils had a considerable audience when the windows were opened. Our informant Georg Thaa, a fellow student of Schubert's at the Stadtkonvikt, tells us that the sound often attracted people returning home from a stroll in the city ... Schubert had already made a bold start at composing. Without question these cheerful and well-organized amateur activities gave him a considerable stimulus and contributed largely to his practical versatility.' Schubert is often called 'self-taught' but he seems to have learned a lot at the Stadtkonvikt.

In 1813, when he was sixteen, Schubert left the Stadtkonvikt and spent a year at the St Anna Teachers' Training College in Vienna. It has been suggested that he was going to be a schoolmaster to avoid military conscription but that is improbable. Schubert, according to an official document, was only 1·57 metres tall (five foot one inch), too short to be accepted by

Schubert aged 16, by
Kupelwieser.

the army. After a year at the Teachers' College he joined his father's school
as an assistant and was put in charge of the youngest, six-year-old children.
It was his father's wish that Franz should have a 'solid' profession. Father
Schubert had started his school with few pupils and only one assistant. But
by 1805 he had almost 300 pupils and six assistants. Many pupils were given
private lessons.

Schubert's father was aware of his son's astonishing musical talent, but
he said Franz could always have his music after working hours in school.
Outstanding talent was not considered sufficient in Father Schubert's
middle-class circles. Since the Austrian state bankruptcy in 1810 there were
not many wealthy music lovers left, and the aristocratic patrons who had
subsidized Beethoven were disappearing. Father Schubert, like so many
fathers, believed in 'Safety First'. And he admittedly liked the idea of his

51

opposite Schubert's
mother Anna.

sons, Ferdinand and Franz, continuing in his own profession, which had brought him some security and middle-class respectability. Music was all right as a hobby, after working hours.

Such an attitude was bound to create conflict. Spaun remembers that Schubert had violent arguments with his father. Spaun speaks on one occasion of a 'storm'. Some biographers claim that during a certain time Schubert was forbidden to live at home, but Deutsch states that such a *Hausverbot* never happened. Possibly in order to forget his troubles Schubert began to write *Lieder* – the sort of music that brought him his greatest fame. Between 1813 and 1816 he wrote some 400 different works, despite the lack of space in Säulengasse and the large number of pupils. Even then he was restless. He would run up and down the Himmelpfort Stairway and with his brothers he would visit the tavern Zum Kreuz (At the Cross). He went there for the last time on 31 October 1828, a few weeks before his death, and was served fish that gave him nausea. It may have been the cause of his fatal illness.

On 30 March 1811, a few weeks after his fourteenth birthday, Schubert wrote *Hagars Klage*, now known as his first *Lied*, though he had probably experimented before. *Hagars Klage* betrays the influence of Johann Rudolf Zumsteeg, a friend of Friedrich Schiller. Zumsteeg set some ballads to music and was also famous as a composer of strophic songs. Schubert found his works probably at the Stadtkonvikt. There he also read Klopstock, Schiller and Goethe; even then he was an avid reader. He wrote a few other songs, among them *Des Mädchens Klage*, after a text by Schiller. His father was not pleased with the young man's activities. Spaun writes that Schubert in those months was 'always earnest and not very cheerful'. Schubert was fascinated by Schiller whose poetry has been called 'impossible' for setting to music. Schubert set forty-two Schiller texts to music, and some are very famous. He created his own style for Schiller's ballads, far beyond what Zumsteeg and others had done. It has been suggested that Schubert might have developed some music-dramatic talent if he had lived later; both Verdi and Wagner were born sixteen years after the death of Schubert. But Schubert would have studied Gluck and Mozart if he had felt the urge to do so. Essentially, like Beethoven, he was not a musical dramatist and his operas were failures. Schubert's greatest gifts were lyrical, his sense of melody, his development of the *Lied*.

His mother died on 28 May 1812, at a time when the young boy was already having arguments with his father. There is some mention of a 'reconciliation' between father and son 'at the grave of the mother' but it may be sentimental invention; at any rate it did not last. Schubert's handwritten remark on a piece of music paper says, 'Started counterpoint on 18 June 1812.'

He had, of course, studied counterpoint much earlier at the Stadtkonvikt. But on 24 September Schubert composed Schiller's *Der Jüngling am Bache*, now considered the first *real* Schubert *Lied*. He was getting involved in his music and very impatient with his six-year-old pupils. 'It is true,' he admitted later, 'that they irritated me whenever I tried to create, and I lost the idea. Naturally I would beat them up.'

He was seventeen and he had discovered the magic of the *Lied*. He set twenty-four poems by Friedrich von Matthison from Germany, an economist by profession and poet by vocation. Then Spaun brought Johann Mayrhofer to Schubert. Mayrhofer, ten years older, became a close friend. He too was a poet by vocation; a dilettante, but Schubert was attracted by his poetry. Mayrhofer once told Grillparzer that his poems seemed good to him only after Schubert had set them to music.

Schubert's development as a composer of songs cannot be rationally explained. His predecessors in Vienna – Gluck, Haydn, Mozart, Beethoven – had created the substance of classicism in music: instrumental music, chamber music, operas, church music, symphonies. Not one had bothered with the kind of song which Schubert created, the *Lied*. Mozart had written songs that almost sound like his versions of an Italian canzonetta. Mozart's finest song, *Das Veilchen*, is not a *Lied* in the sense of Schubert's *Lieder*. Mozart always wrote for the singing voice but he was a dramatist at heart and even his great concert arias are musical drama. Beethoven wrote great classical songs, but not *Lieder*. It remained for Schubert to create a new art form which he developed almost from its very beginning to the greatest perfection. Haydn did this with the string quartet; he was twenty-three when he wrote his first quartet and he was in his seventies when he wrote his last great masterpieces. Schubert had less time for the evolution of his speciality. He was fourteen when he wrote his first *Lieder* and only just thirty-one when he composed his last songs.

1814 remains an important year. On 19 October Schubert wrote his first masterpiece *Gretchen am Spinnrade*, 'Meine Ruh' ist hin, mein Herz ist schwer', from Goethe's *Faust*. It shows the unmistakable genius of Schubert, the miraculous fusion of words and sounds, of poetry and music. Schubert ends each of the three parts of the *Lied* with Gretchen's outcry 'Meine Ruh' ist hin', which is not exactly the way Goethe wrote it – but it is perfect. Had Schubert done nothing else he would be immortal today.

Seven years later, in 1821, his friends the Sonnleithners published *Gretchen am Spinnrade* privately with the opus number 2. (Op. 1 is *Erlkönig* which Schubert wrote a year after *Gretchen*.) Schubert dedicated the song to the Swiss-born banker Count Moritz von Fries and received a 'gratification' of 20 ducats. Not a great deal of money but his friends were excited about *Gretchen am Spinnrade*. Even Salieri seems to have changed his mind about the former pupil for he exclaimed, 'He (Schubert) is a genius. He can do anything he wants!'

Schubert's Goethe songs – he set over seventy of Goethe's poems to music – are among his greatest. Schubert understood the greatness of Goethe. Goethe did not understand Schubert at all. Late in 1814 Schubert composed Goethe's *Nachtgesang* and *Sehnsucht*. Spaun and two other friends from the Stadtkonvikt, Anton Holzapfel and Albert Stadler, were getting excited about Schubert. They and two other friends, Franz von Schober and Anselm Hüttenbrenner, would meet in Schubert's family home. His father did not like to see the boys there. He said they were having 'a bad influence' on Franz, the young school teacher. From his point of view, he was probably right.

On Sunday afternoons the boys went back into the Stadtkonvikt. Stadler remembered later on that they were not exactly welcome there either, and had to join the afternoon service at the nearby church 'which took over half an hour'. Schubert did not have to go there. 'We locked him up in one of the rooms (of the Stadtkonvikt), gave him music paper and a volume with poetry, anything we happened to have with us. When we returned from the church service, he usually had written something which he let me have.'

Stadler began to copy Schubert's songs. We owe to him many that might otherwise have been lost. Schubert was often careless about his manuscripts. He would write a song, give it to a friend and forget about it; he knew he could always write another one. Spaun remembers: 'In 1812 he composed twelve minuets and trios of extraordinary beauty ... Schubert lent these minuets from one person to another, and they vanished and no one knew who had had them last. He was upset but too vexed to write them out again, he put it off and finally they slipped from memory ...' The exact number of the *Lieder* he wrote is still unknown. There may be more still to be discovered.

After a new *Lied* was finished Holzapfel might sing it – he had a particularly good voice – and Schubert might accompany him at the piano. Stadler writes about Schubert's piano playing, 'Nice touch, steady hand, a clear pleasant way of playing, full of spirit and sentiment. He belonged to the old class of piano players who do not use their fingers like hammers on the keys.' Anselm Hüttenbrenner wrote: 'Schubert also played the violin and the viola, he read all keys with the same facility ... His voice was weak but very *gemütlich*. In his nineteenth year he sang baritone and tenor. If needed,

One of Schubert's
earliest friends, Anselm
Hüttenbrenner.

when no woman was available, he would also sing the alto and soprano part,
when they sang old scores from the Court Library under Salieri.'

As time went on Schubert became less interested in Schiller – he composed
a few more of Schiller's poems before 1818, the last in 1823 – and more in
Goethe. He was artistically mature at an early age as though he sensed he
did not have much time. 'Schubert found everything in Goethe's poems that
he tried to express in music,' Fischer-Dieskau writes. 'Clarity of thought,
unequivocal expression, deep sensitivity, an imaginative language.' Sometimes Schubert wrote several versions of the same poem; he was getting self-
critical. He wrote three versions of *Des Mädchens Klage* and two of Goethe's
Nähe des Geliebten. Much of Schubert's best music is sad music. Once he asked,
'Do you know any really cheerful music? I don't know any.' There is some

Schiller, whose poems the young Schubert set to music.

cheerful music – one thinks of Haydn, Mozart, Rossini, Verdi, Johann Strauss – but Schubert was a romantic who loved music for its sadness.

In 1815, a memorable year in Schubert's life, he wrote some 150 *Lieder*. Rossini once boasted he could set a laundry list to music. Schubert, it has been said, might have composed a menu; it would have been a melodious meal. On 19 August he composed six Goethe poems, among them *Heidenröslein* ('Sah ein Knab' ein Röslein stehn') that has become so popular – a folk song – that the composer is almost anonymous. The poem has been set by other composers but none achieved Schubert's simple beauty. On 16 November Schubert set Goethe's *Erlkönig* to music. For a hundred years after his death it was considered his greatest *Lied*. Spaun later thought he remembered how the masterpiece was created.

conclusion

57

We found Schubert all excited, reading aloud *Erlkönig* from a book. He walked up and down, suddenly he sat down, and in a very short time the wonderful ballad was on paper. Since Schubert had no piano, we ran into the Stadtkonvikt, and there *Erlkönig* was sung the same evening and enthusiastically received.

Some Schubert scholars, among them J.E. Brown, refuse to believe that the ballad was set in such a short time. But Schubert was a fast worker and he avoided repeating all phrases in the accompaniment. Benedikt Randhartinger, his former classmate, remembered in 1888 that he first sang *Erlkönig* at the Stadtkonvikt with Schubert himself at the piano.

Schubert, very modest, said, 'Benedictus, the song pleases me too, if only it were not so difficult to play.' The second time, Schubert omitted the triplets and replaced them by quavers. Some of the teachers asked him why he omitted the triplets and he replied, 'They are too difficult for me, a virtuoso might play them.' The honorarium for this and other performances consisted, apart from enthusiasm, in presents of music paper, which the students gave Schubert so he might be able to compose more.

The anecdote has a true ring. Many composers have written music which they regretfully were unable to perform. Richard Strauss once apologized to Helene Wildbrunn, after a rehearsal of *Elektra*, for writing such difficult vocal parts, saying, 'I'm sorry I had to put in these high Cs – I know Richard Wagner would have achieved the same effect with a B flat.'

What matters is not the technical difficulty but the miracle that an eighteen-year-old youth turned Goethe's ballad, originally written in 1782 for the Singspiel *Die Fischerin*, into a masterpiece of musical imagination. Many composers have written their version of *Erlkönig* – Beethoven wrote a sketch of the music but abandoned the effort – yet none approaches Schubert's depth of feeling.

Schubert did not care that others had set 'his' poems to music; he had the glorious innocence and courage of youth. Some forty composers have tried to set Goethe's *An den Mond* ('Füllest wieder Busch und Tal'). Schubert tried two versions in 1815. The second, written shortly before *Erlkönig*, is very beautiful. People have said it would be impossible to set this poem to music because Goethe's words are almost pure music, but Schubert did.

He tried to compose Goethe's *Kennst du das Land* from *Mignon*, and gave up: he knew his song was not as good as Beethoven's. Robert Schumann also tried to set it twice and wrote, 'Apart from Beethoven's, I know no single setting of this song which matches in the slightest degree the impression that this poem makes without music ... Let Beethoven tell you whence he produced his music.'

Schubert wrote five different versions of Goethe's *Mignon und der Harfner* (Mignon and the Harper), 'Nur wer die Sehnsucht kennt.' The first, in F major, written in 1815 is perhaps the best. Schubert kept thinking of this *Lied* for almost eleven years, during his whole adult life. There is your 'fast' or 'sloppy' worker. Nothing about Schubert is simple and unequivocal.

Early in 1816 Schubert applied for the position of a music teacher at the German Normal School in Laibach (now Ljubljana in Yugoslavia). According to the official *Wiener Zeitung* the applicant 'should be a well learned singer, organist and violin player, know the usual woodwind and brass instruments, and have the ability of teaching'. It may have seemed like a god-sent opportunity to get away from his job at his father's school. Schubert also hoped to make more money there. In his application he emphasized, not too wisely, that he had 'such experience in the field of composition and in playing the organ, the violin and singing, that he is, according to the enclosed reports, among all applicants the best suited'. He may have quoted letters from Salieri and Domherr Josef Spendou that he enclosed. He failed to get the job which was given to a local music teacher in Laibach.

Josef von Spaun.

But Schubert decided to give up living with his family, and leave his job as his father's assistant. The quiet and modest man felt that he had to be on his own, away from his father's restrictions and the drudgery of the job he hated. The difficult decision is characteristic of Schubert who could be tough towards himself. But he had confidence and even though he was going to give up the secure life to try to prove himself as a musician he could always count on his friends' support.

Musically it was a time of indecision. Fragmentary entries in his diary show that Schubert was low, often depressed. Goethe had not responded to a letter from Spaun with a package containing Schubert's finest Goethe songs, among them *Gretchen am Spinnrade* and *Erlkönig*. Schubert wrote three sonatas Op. 137, better known as sonatinas, for violin and piano. Though the treatment has been called 'amateurish', the sonatinas are lovely expressions of Schubert's charm, seemingly simple yet difficult to perform in their simplicity. He wrote the String Quartet in E major Op. 125, No. 2, which is not like the early quartets he wrote for domestic use though not yet a masterpiece. It is technically difficult and contains moments of virtuoso writing which Schubert later on carefully omitted. He wrote the C minor (Tragic) Symphony that shows the influence of Beethoven's *Coriolanus* Overture and of *Egmont*. He was feeling his way. He wrote the beautiful Mass in C major which he dedicated to his former teacher, Michael Holzer. He was not yet where he wanted to be but he sensed he was getting there.

Friends, Always Friends

Schubert was nineteen when he made a complete break with convention and middle-class life. He had his freedom and would live only for his music. But he had no fixed income, no security. He was lucky to be supported by his friends, who were faithful and generous though most of them were not rich. They believed in him, they cheered him up when he was depressed, they inspired him. They sensed something about his talent though they had no idea of his true genius. But how could anyone divine the real Schubert, the sensitive romanticist with the gift of melody who becomes almost mystical in his late masterpieces when he approaches the dark power and limitless space that Beethoven reached in his absolute music, the late string quartets. That was the side of Schubert the friends did not know. They were fond of 'Schwammerl' who would sit down at the piano, improvising some dances.

Schubert was often misunderstood but he made no conscious attempt to be understood. We know him now because we listen to his music. Our judgement is not clouded by personal acquaintance. His friends never overcame this handicap. Fifty years after his death when they were old, writing their reminiscences, they unwillingly created the romantic legend of Franz Schubert.

Most of his friends were poets and dilettante writers who loved the magic atmosphere of romanticism that was so different from their routine middle-class lives. We know the friends from Schubert's letters – he wrote illuminating letters with precise details – and from their letters and diaries. They cared about Schubert and they admired him. They thought he was a sweet fellow but they would have been surprised by his greatness that was first revealed fifty-six years after his death when publication of the Complete Edition of Schubert's Works began after 1884.

According to O.E. Deutsch 74 letters that Schubert wrote have survived. (From Mozart we have some 350 letters, from Beethoven almost 1500.) Schubert wrote seven poems, one allegorical story, two fragmentary diaries, thirty-five characteristic dedications and personal notes on his manuscripts.

opposite Schubert with his friends Hüttenbrenner and Jenger.

A Schubert evening at Josef von Spaun's. Schubert is seated at the piano with Vogl singing. The portrait on the wall is of Caroline Esterhazy.

We also have fifty letters written to Schubert, and 230 letter quotations and 300 diary quotations about him. At least three diaries written by friends, Anselm Hüttenbrenner, Leopold von Sonnleithner, and Johann Baptist Jenger were destroyed, perhaps wilfully.

Schubert's friends were more or less his age. They were young and Schubert himself never grew old. His music is melodious and youthful, and yet in his melancholy moments he expresses the sufferings of youth. Some of his former classmates at the Stadtkonvikt in Vienna came from the provinces, especially from Upper Austria. They studied at the University or had just started their professional careers, and they talked a great deal about Schubert and wrote to each other about him. Some were painters, and they painted Schubert and the other friends. They may seem a relaxed crowd, always singing and dancing and their girls were pretty in their high-waisted long dresses. They would make excursions in the countryside or sit in wine gardens; superficially they convey the image of a Biedermeier idyl. No wonder, since most of the paintings were made much later when the artists remembered their earlier 'idyllic' years with a sharp sense of nostalgia.

Schubert's friends occupy a unique position in his life. Other men of genius had friends who supported, stimulated and occasionally criticized them which is also a sort of stimulation. Schubert's friends became almost his family, a substitute for the love which he rarely knew. Except for certain intervals, when Schubert went back home, he stayed with his friends or lived alone for twelve years as a guest, or subtenant, always composing, never trying hard to get his works before a large public. He was satisfied with the small audience of his friends. They had their arguments but Schubert was never seriously hurt by any of them. He often reconciled arguments among them. 'Through Schubert we all became friends and brothers,' Spaun remembered much later.

Paradoxically Schubert had both modesty and a healthy sense of self-confidence. Bauernfeld writes that two well-known members of the Vienna Opera orchestra once came to the coffeehouse table where he and Schubert sat, and asked if Schubert would write a new piece for their concert, with solo passages. Schubert refused.

And when they said they were among the best artists in Vienna, Schubert said, 'Artists? Musical hacks you are, nothing else. One of you bites at the brass mouthpiece of his wooden stick, and the other blows out his cheeks at the horn. Do you call that art? It's a trade, a knack that earns money, and nothing else. I am Franz Schubert whom everybody knows and recognizes. I am not just a composer of *Ländler*, as the stupid newspapers say and the stupid people repeat. I am Franz Schubert, and don't you forget it.'

This is the other Schubert, not so well known as the cheerful companion who liked good talk and good music, a few friends and a glass of wine.

Anselm Hüttenbrenner wrote:

His musical judgements were acute, concise and to the point and he always hit the nail on the head. In this he was like Beethoven who now and then was given to irony. When at social gatherings some presumptuous amateur put forward assertions, Schubert told him, 'Better say nothing, you don't understand it and you never will.' He liked to converse about Handel, Mozart and Beethoven and thought highly of the two Haydns. With Bach's compositions he was only slightly conversant. It was Beethoven's Mass in C major that most of all moved him to devotion.

Schubert did not dance but he composed and played dances for his friends. Then one of the young poets would read his latest poem and if Schubert was attracted by it he might set it to music right away. He instinctively responded to all kinds of poetry, whether it was by Goethe or Heine, or a dilettante such as Mayrhofer or Schober. Franz von Schober, one of his closest friends, contributed twelve poems to Schubert's life work. Schober's *An die Musik* ('Du holde Kunst melodisch süsser Klagen') was very popular with the friends and remains one of the immortal Schubert songs. The composer loved it and made several copies of the original. One, now kept at the Conservatoire de Paris, has Schubert's handwritten remark, 'Manuscrit très precieux'. Obviously he knew his value.

Schubert was not comfortable on the rare occasions when he found himself in high society. He preferred the company of simple people and congenial friends. He loved the *Würstelbälle*, where *Würstel* (Frankfurters) and beer

right The house at
Atzenbrugg.

below The garden-house
at Atzenbrugg.

were served. His friends would listen to a new *Lied* he had written, and they would write to their girls and to other friends in Upper Austria. They might send a copy of the new composition there and thus the circle would grow. The girls often came from middle-class homes where everybody loved music. The young people played games and charades, they laughed or talked seriously about life and themselves. 'Schwammerl' was always the focus of these gatherings which they called *Schubertiaden*.

A coloured sketch of a *Schubertiade* by Ludwig Mohn, made around 1820 (after a drawing by Franz von Schober, who made the landscape and architecture, and Moritz von Schwind, who drew the figures), is now at the Austrian National Library. Called *The Feast at Atzenbrugg* it shows Castle Atzenbrugg, in the vicinity of Vienna, where Schober's uncle was steward. After 1817 the friends would make an annual excursion there and stay three days. Schubert is seated in shirt-sleeves in the foreground, smoking a pipe, with Schober next to him. Another Schubertian, the landscape painter and musician Kraissl, plays the fiddle. Young men and girls listen and some play ball. It is a perfect idyl – if such a thing exists.

At that time Vienna had over eighty coffeehouses serving real coffee, which had been unavailable until 1813 during Napoleon's Continental Blockade. Vienna had five theatres. The two court theatres were the Hoftheater near the Burg (the Burgtheater) and the Hoftheater near the Kärntnertor, not far from today's Opera, where mostly Italian opera was performed. The three private theatres were in the suburbs: the Theater an der Wien, built by Schikaneder where Beethoven's *Fidelio* was first heard in 1805; the Theater in der Leopoldstadt; and the Theater in der Josefstadt. The Theater an der Wien and the Theater in der Josefstadt, for a while known as Reinhardt Theater, are still there, occasionally flourishing. In 1976 the Burgtheater celebrated its 200th anniversary. The present State Opera is an upstart, relatively speaking. The beautiful House on the Ring was opened in 1869.

Concerts, in Schubert's time, were given at the Redoutensäle of the Hofburg, the festival hall of the University, the Landhaus Saal, the hall of the Society of the Friends of Music in Tuchlauben, and the Hotel zum Römischen Kaiser. Tickets cost from one to two florins. And people loved to dance.

The Griensteidl coffeehouse.

69

The Theater an der Wien in 1830.

The Prince de Ligne, who might otherwise have been forgotten, is remembered for his *bon mot* about the Congress of Vienna, '*Le Congrès ne marche pas – il dance*'. During the *Fasching* (Carnival) in 1821 there were over 1600 public balls in Vienna. Three years later Johann Strauss the Younger was born. His early waltzes were influenced by Schubert, by Joseph Lanner, and by his father.

It was said that there was a piano in every cultured home in Vienna. Many aristocrats had given up their private orchestras but the well-to-do people went to concerts and listened to outdoor performances. Some people had more than one piano. The banker Johann Heinrich von Geymüller, one of Schubert's few wealthy patrons, had five in his home, one for each of his daughters. The Emperor had his own string quartet but unlike many Habsburgs he did not really love music. There was regular *Hausmusik* in the homes of many middle-class people where chamber music and piano music were performed. The piano manufacturers (Bösendorfer) and the music publishers (Artaria) would arrange concerts. The populace at large enjoyed the *Harmoniemusik* of military bands in streets and squares, the string ensembles of Johann Strauss the Elder and Joseph Lanner, the harp players in the Prater, the organ grinders everywhere, and the musical clocks on many buildings. After the Second Turkish Siege in 1683 Abraham a Sancta Clara,

70

a popular preacher, had said that 'music resounded from noblemen's houses and courtyards'; around 1825 there was music everywhere. Vienna was truly 'the world capital of music' which nowadays it only pretends to be.

Some of Schubert's early instrumental music was written for groups of cultured dilettantes and music lovers. Leopold von Sonnleithner has written about Otto Hatwig's small orchestra. They played first at the Schottenhof and after 1818 at the Gundelhof, and performed the symphonies of Haydn, Mozart, the first two by Beethoven, and overtures by Cherubini, Spontini, Méhul, Boieldieu. Expenses were defrayed by modest subscriptions from the participants. Otto Hatwig was concert-master and Schubert's brother, Ferdinand, was among the first violinists; Schubert was the first viola player, and Peter Edler von Decret played percussion. 'Apart from a few professional musicians, most of the gentlemen belonged to the merchant-tradesman or minor-official class.' The concerts, modestly called 'musical practices', became well known and tickets had to be issued, though the rooms had space for 120 listeners. Some of Schubert's works, among them his First Symphony, were first performed there.

Financially these performances were not rewarding. The small musical groups could not afford to pay fees to a composer. Schubert's first fee of 100 florins was paid for his Cantata *Prometheus*, commissioned by the students and friends of Professor Heinrich Josef Watteroth on his name day in 1816.

The Party Game of the Schubertians at Atzenbrugg, acting out a charade.

A musical evening,
showing Schubert,
Bauernfeld,
Kupelwieser, the Frölich
sisters, Moritz von
Schwind, Josef von
Spaun, Vogl,
Grillparzer.

Franz von Schober.

He was popular with his students for his nonconformist views. (The Prometheus theme is perhaps significant; Prometheus rebelled against Olympus and defied the punishment of the gods.) At that time Schubert and Spaun stayed at the suburb Landstrasse 97, in the house owned by Professor Wateroth.

The favourite meeting places of the Schubertians are known. Around 1822 they patronized the Hotel Zur Ungarischen Krone in Seilerstätte, the tavern Zum Anker in Grünangergasse, and Bogner's Coffeehouse in Singerstrasse. Some of Schubert's works were first performed in public at the Hotel Zum römischen Kaiser in Renngasse.

Perhaps the closest of Schubert's friends was Franz von Schober, one year older, born in Sweden of a German father and an Austrian mother; he had met Schubert through Spaun. He was a wealthy dilettante, the first who offered Schubert a place to stay. When he was in Vienna – he was restless and moved around a lot – Schubert could always count on staying with him. Schober later became private secretary to Franz Liszt, *Legationsrat* in Weimar, married when he was sixty and died in 1882 in Dresden. Strangely enough, Schober is the only one of Schubert's close friends who did not write a set of reminiscences about him.

Joseph von Spaun, nine years older than Schubert, studied law, went as a civil servant to Lemberg, Galicia and in 1841 became director of the Austrian State Lottery. After Schubert's death he wrote to Bauernfeld that 'Schubert should be treated as a song composer by his biographers. We shall never make a Mozart or Haydn out of him in instrumental and church composition whereas in song he is unsurpassed.' Spaun inherited from Wilhelm Witteczek – another Schubertian who copied and saved many of Schubert's songs – his collection of printed and written copies and bequeathed it to the Gesellschaft der Musikfreunde.

And there was Johann Mayrhofer from Steyr, Upper Austria, amateur poet and law student in Vienna, a passionate believer in freedom, who paradoxically became a censor. Deutsch describes him as 'taciturn, sarcastic, and a misogynist'. Schubert was fond of him, stayed with him on several occasions and set some of Mayrhofer's poems to music. Mayrhofer died soon after Schubert: in 1836 he jumped from an upper window of his office.

Moritz von Schwind (1796–1882) joined the Schubertians after 1820. He later became a noted painter, liked musical subjects, and decorated the lunettes of the loggias in the foyer of the Vienna Opera with poetically conceived reproductions of scenes from *Die Zauberflöte*. (The foyer was the only part of the opera house that survived the bombs and the fire at the end of the Second World War; Schwind's decorations are still there.) Seven years

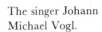

The singer Johann
Michael Vogl.

after Schubert's death Schwind planned to paint a 'Schubert room', with
each wall dedicated to an important poet of Schubert's *Lieder*, but the plan
was not executed. In 1868 he did a sepia drawing *Ein Schubert Abend bei Ritter
von Spaun* (A Schubert Evening at Ritter von Spaun) which now belongs
to the City of Vienna. 'It shows my excellent friend Franz Schubert at the
piano with a circle of listeners, old Vogl singing, and the whole company,
men and women around.'

Johann Michael Vogl (1768–1840), older than Schubert, became an important member of the circle. He too was from Steyr, a professional singer
who in 1794 became a member of the Vienna Court Opera. He retired in
1822, but continued to sing privately. Vogl met Schubert through Schober
in 1817. At the beginning of their relationship the celebrated singer treated
the unknown composer with some condescension. Spaun remembers that

Vogl once told Schubert, 'there is something in you but you are too little of a comedian, too little of a charlatan, you squander your fine thoughts without making the best of them'. A cartoon, probably drawn by Schober, shows the singer walking in front, proud and arrogant, and little Schubert three steps behind him, with some music under his arm and some in his back pocket.

Vogl did much for Schubert though. A few weeks after he had met the composer he sang *Erlkönig*, *Ganymed* and other *Lieder* for the friends. Later he performed Schubert's songs in public which was unusual: there were no song recitals in those days. 'The enthusiasm with which the great artist sang these songs was proof of how much he liked them,' wrote Spaun. 'The singer had influence upon the composer who was happy to see his long-dreamed wishes fulfilled. The friendship lasted until Schubert's death. Vogl supplied the treasure of his practical experiences ...' Sonnleithner remembered that Vogl sang many Schubert *Lieder* with excitement and emotion 'but in his later years with definite affectation and a certain complacency. Schubert had to set his songs especially for him ... The complaint that Schubert's *Lieder* are not always written for a certain vocal range (*Stimmlage*) is due to the influence of Vogl.' Schubert did not think of his interpreters when he wrote his songs. He wrote his music as he felt it, making no compromise with himself or others. Many of his *Lieder* are difficult to sing because of the way they are set, with extraordinarily high or low notes.

In his *Family Chronicle* (1876) Franz von Hartmann writes about a *Schubertiade* at Spaun's when Vogl sang some thirty songs more beautifully than ever. 'There were among others Frau von Arneth, Grillparzer, Kupelwieser, Mayrhofer, and his landlord "lanky Hubert" – the ugliest person I ever saw whom Schwind portrayed with a few strokes.' Spaun remembers that Vogl sang the *Winterreise* cycle first at Schober's.

We were dumbfounded by the gloomy mood of these songs but Schubert said, 'I like these songs more than all the others and you will get to like them too', and he was right ... More beautiful German songs probably do not exist. When publishers told Schubert that people found the accompaniment to his songs too hard and the keys too difficult, that he ought to pay attention to this, Schubert always replied that he could not write differently and that anyone who could not play his compositions should leave them alone ... Schubert's music must either be performed well or not at all.

That applies to all good music though. Schubert's image, emerging from the memories of his friends, is that of a complex, sympathetic, always very real human being, a difficult man and an honest artist.

Ferdinand Hiller, the composer and writer on music who went with Hummel to Vienna, wrote in 1879 in his *Vienna 52 Years Ago*, 'Schubert had

opposite Schober's cartoon of Schubert and Vogl.

Vogl und *Franz Schubert ziehen aus zu Kampf und Sieg.*

right Schubert and Vogl
at the piano.

only little technique, Vogl had but little voice, but both had so much life
and feeling and were so completely absorbed in their performances that the
wonderful compositions could not have been performed with greater clarity
and greater vision.'
Sonnleithner wrote:

When Schubert accompanied his own songs he always kept strict and even time,
except when he had indicated ritardando, accelerando etc. He never allowed violent
expressions in performance. The *Lieder* singer as a rule relates the experiences and
feelings of others, he does not himself impersonate the characters whose feelings he
describes. Poet, composer, and singer must conceive the song lyrically, not dramatically. With Schubert the true expression is already inherent in the melody and is
admirably enhanced by the accompaniment.

Sonnleithner, who never liked Vogl, thought that Karl Freiherr von Schönstein, one of Schubert's few aristocratic friends, was perhaps the best
Schubert singer of his day.

Schönstein himself had much admiration for Vogl.

Schubert would bring his creations to Meister Vogl and was ready to take his advice.
Once, after Vogl had sung a Schubert *Lied* without the slightest change – occasionally he would take liberties with Schubert's songs – Schubert exclaimed, 'You know,
that song isn't bad! Who wrote it?' After a couple of weeks, he no longer recognized
his own *Lied*.

opposite A drawing by
Kupelwieser.

78

Vogl may have had his faults – he was an egocentric singer – but he was a good influence upon Schubert. When Schubert, who did not consider social obligations important, failed to appear at a party he had promised to attend, Vogl would defend him. 'We must bow to his genius. If he doesn't come we ought to crawl after him on our knees.' This is no longer the arrogant singer who would precede Schubert by three steps.

After Vogl died his widow, perhaps trying to get attention, quoted her husband. 'Vogl believed that Schubert was in a somnambulistic state whenever he wrote music. This explains how, in this visionary condition, the scarcely educated boy could see into the secrets of life, have the emotions, the knowledge.' This nonsense could be ignored but it was later repeated by others and added another false touch to the Schubert legend. He was very much awake and always himself whenever he wrote music.

Other members of Schubert's circle were Albert Stadler, from the Steyr district, and Wilhelm Witteczek, who copied many Schubert manuscripts. There was the painter Leopold Kupelwieser and his brother Josef who wrote the libretto for Schubert's opera *Fierabras*. It was not performed in Schubert's lifetime; neither was *Alfonso und Estrella*, written by Schober.

Franz Grillparzer, Austria's greatest playwright who felt he was 'too old' because he was six years older than Schubert, was never a member of the inner circle of friends. But in his autobiography he confessed he would have liked to have belonged to the Schubertians. 'We founded an Academy of Sciences, we held meetings every week at which lectures were read. In order that the whole thing should not become too serious, we founded at the same time a comic journal in which we all printed much nonsense by our academicians or other members.' Grillparzer dedicated to Schubert a poem that begins:

The playwright Franz Grillparzer.

> Lobt mich – es soll mich freuen
> Schmäht mich – ich muss es dulden.
> Schubert heiss ich, Schubert bin ich...
> (Praise me – I shall be pleased
> Spurn me – I shall endure it.
> I am Schubert, and Schubert I remain.)

It would seem that the sensitive poet understood Schubert better than the other friends. But even Grillparzer did not really comprehend the greatness of Schubert, otherwise he would never have written the famous epitaph, 'The art of music here interred a rich possession/But far fairer hopes still.' Fairer hopes? Schubert, the composer of some of the greatest songs, beautiful chamber music, the wonderful symphonies? One cannot say that this work was incomplete.

Schubert's Wohnhaus
im Jahre 1818
in Zseliz

Schubert set only three Grillparzer poems to music. He may have kept a respectful distance knowing that Grillparzer belonged to the circle around Beethoven. Schubert was with Bauernfeld at Beethoven's funeral. Heinrich Anschütz, the popular Burgtheater actor, spoke Grillparzer's words, 'The last master of the lyrical *Lied* . . . is no longer with us.' Schubert may have wondered if this were so.

Grillparzer, already famous after the success of his plays *Die Ahnfrau* (1817) and *Sappho* (1818), probably met Schubert in the house of the banker Heinrich von Geymüller. There, according to a widespread Biedermeier story, Grillparzer fell in love with Katharina (Katty) Fröhlich, the third of four musically gifted daughters of a suburban manufacturer, who were often at the Geymüllers'. The four Fröhlich girls were good singers, from soprano to mezzo to contralto. Katty did not become a professional singer but 'she got herself drunk on good music as a drunkard does on wine', Grillparzer wrote. He first admired the older two girls but eventually fell in love with Katty and became engaged to her for a few years, though they never got married. Grillparzer remained attached to her and to the whole family. The only daughter to get married was the second girl, Barbara; she married the flautist Ferdinand Bogner, whom Schubert knew well. Anna Fröhlich taught singing at the Conservatory of the Gesellschaft der Musikfreunde, Josephine became an opera singer, and Katty is remembered as Grillparzer's 'eternal betrothed'.

At the request of Louise Gosmar, a pupil of Anna Fröhlich, Grillparzer wrote a poem for a serenade for Louise's birthday celebration. Grillparzer's beautiful *Ständchen* was set to music by Schubert who changed Grillparzer's beginning, 'Zögernd stille', to *Zögernd leise* Op. 135. (According to another version the idea came from Anna Fröhlich who wanted a surprise for her pupil.) Schubert originally wrote it for Anna's sister, Josephine, and a male chorus. Sonnleithner writes, 'Schubert took the poem, went into an alcove by the window, read it through carefully a few times and said with a smile, "I've got it already, it's done, and it's going to be quite good."' After a couple of days Schubert returned with the composition. 'It really was quite good,' Sonnleithner wrote thirty years later. Schubert had set Grillparzer's *Ständchen* for contralto and male chorus, and Anna Frölich was upset; her pupils were girls, not men. Schubert did not mind. He simply made another version for soprano and female chorus, and Anna Fröhlich, an important person in Vienna's musical life, was pleased. The serenade was sung on 11 August 1827, Louise Gosmar's birthday, in the garden of the Langs' house in Döbling where Beethoven had once stayed. A piano was even taken into the garden after dark, and everyone was happy. A few

opposite The elaborate painting *Die Symphonie* by Moritz von Schwind.

The Frölich sisters (left to right) Betty, Katharina and Anna. Katharina ('Katty') was Grillparzer's 'eternal betrothed'.

months later, the *Ständchen* was performed during a concert of the Philharmonic Society, and Schubert was brought there by his friends. Later he said to Anna Fröhlich, 'You know, I never realized how beautiful it was.' It is beautiful, especially the earlier version for contralto and male chorus.

Grillparzer's affection for Katty Fröhlich and his sad old age as a bitter, eccentric bachelor are no Biedermeier story but part of Austria's literary history. In his younger years he had called her 'the girl with the eyes', and in one poem describes her 'as she sat listening'. Theodor von Karajan, Grillparzer's friend, tells us that Katty had 'immense eyes, bottomless, really unfathomable'. Was Schubert the pianist, while Katty 'sat listening'? Deutsch dismisses the possibility as 'merely a tradition'. But Schubert liked the *Ständchen* so much that he put it on the programme of his only Private Concert, a few months before his death.

The Sonnleithners too were helpful friends. They were an old, patrician family and somehow they come close to Beethoven's aristocratic patrons. Joseph Sonnleithner was the clumsy librettist of Beethoven's *Fidelio*. His sister, a hyper-sensitive woman who later had depressions and committed suicide, was the mother of Franz Grillparzer. Joseph's brother, Dr Ignaz

Sonnleithner, tried to launch Schubert's early *Lieder* and chamber music. He and his son Leopold arranged private concerts at home. Schubert was often the centre of attraction.

The Sonnleithners also tried to help him earn some money. When *Erlkönig* was sung there and the Schubertians were enthusiastic about it, Leopold Sonnleithner offered the fine *Lied* to two local music publishers, Tobias Haslinger and Antonio Diabelli. Both refused to publish the song, even without a fee. 'The composer was unknown and the piano accompaniment was too difficult, and successful sales could not be expected,' they told Sonnleithner. The eternal publisher's argument. Then Sonnleithner and some friends collected money and had the song published at their own expense. Leopold Sonnleithner recalls:

When at a musical soirée in our house my father announced that *Erlkönig* was now available, about a hundred copies were bought there and then by those present, and the costs of the second publication were covered. Thus we had the first twelve pieces engraved at our expense, and Diabelli sold them on commission. Out of the ample proceeds we paid Schubert's arrears in rent, his debts to the shoemaker, the tailor, the restaurant and the coffeehouse, and could still hand over to him a considerable sum of money. Unfortunately he needed such tutelage, for he had no sense of domestic economy.

Leopold Sonnleithner (*above*) and his uncle Josef (*below*).

He certainly had not. One morning Schwind came to Schubert to take him out on an excursion into the Vienna Woods. Schubert was getting dressed. He looked in his drawers for a pair of socks but every pair was torn to pieces. 'Schwind,' Schubert said with comical seriousness, 'I now really believe that whole ones are not knitted any more.'

Vienna's music publishers were not among Schubert's friends. They wanted from him compositions they could sell easily – pieces that Schubert would not deliver, of course. They bought some of his waltzes, polonaises and marches, and – strangely – the A minor Quartet Op. 29. But most of his instrumental music was not printed while he was alive. Eventually Schubert became bitter about being treated like 'a talented beginner'. The case of *Erlkönig* is typical; that was of course before the Sonnleithners had arranged to have the song printed privately. After he had written the *Lied* his friends in Vienna sent the manuscript to Breitkopf & Härtel, then the most prestigious music publishers, in Leipzig. Gottfried Christoph Härtel sent the manuscript to the composer Franz Schubert (no relation) in Dresden, asking for his evaluation. This Schubert was upset, assuming that someone had used his name. 'It is with the greatest astonishment,' he wrote to Härtel, 'that I have to inform you that this cantata (*sic*) was never written by me.'

In the summer of 1822 Friedrich von Rochlitz, the noted music critic and founder of the *Allgemeine musikalische Zeitung* in Leipzig, wrote a letter to Ignaz von Mosel, an important member of Vienna's musical establishment, calling Schubert's recent work 'estimable'. 'Perhaps this talented artist requires only a scientifically trained friend to enlighten him in a kindly manner about himself ... Then, one hopes, he would discover for himself what he ought to do.' If Rochlitz, a respected musical expert, could write such nonsense about Schubert, one should not be surprised at the ignorant attitude of the public at large. Schubert was lucky to live in Vienna where he was at least admired and loved by his friends. If he knew about Rochlitz, he was not bothered by his pompous attitude. In January 1827 he found three Rochlitz poems he liked – *Alinde, An die Laute, Zur guten Nacht* – and set them to music. Thanks to Schubert the late Rochlitz now finds himself in the company of Goethe and Heine.

Schubert wrote to Breitkopf & Härtel on 12 August 1826 hoping 'that my name is not wholly unknown to you' and asking 'most humbly' whether they would be averse 'to accepting my compositions at reasonable terms'. He offered them songs, string quartets, piano sonatas, four-handed pieces. He would consider it a special honour to be associated with so old and famous an art firm.

Breitkopf & Härtel replied they knew nothing about the 'commercial success' of Schubert's compositions and were unable to offer him any 'fixed pecuniary remuneration'. They might publish some things, giving him a few 'free copies'. The letter might have been written today.

Schubert's first published works, for which he received no payment, were three songs: Mayrhofer's *Am Erlachsee*, Franz Schlechta's *Wiederschein* and Christian Daniel Schubert's *Die Forelle* ('An einem Bächlein helle') that became a celebrated song and the nucleus of Schubert's *Trout* Quintet. The three songs were 'supplements' to the Pocket Books of 1818 and 1829. Diabelli refused to publish *Erlkönig* on commercial terms, but Pietro Cappi, a partner in the firm, promised to publish the songs Op. 1–7 and 12–14 'at the composer's risk', after his friends had agreed to pay the costs of printing. The songs became a success, and Cappi offered Schubert 800 gulden for the plates of the first twelve numbers. That was more money than Schubert had ever been offered, and he accepted without telling his friends; he wanted a little money. His friends were upset, and rightly so: it was only in 1823 Schubert realized that Cappi had taken advantage of him. In an unusually strong letter he asked the publishers to return his manuscripts. Josef Hüttenbrenner went to collect them but he did not get all the manuscripts that Schubert had sent: Cappi & Diabelli kept some *Lieder* and the A minor Sonata.

Schubert now began dealing with another publishing firm, Sauer & Leidesdorf, but they were erratic, undecided and had no money. So Schubert had to go back to Cappi & Diabelli. In his final years he became almost desperate and gave his manuscripts to anyone who expressed some interest – Anton Pennauer, Domenico Artaria and Tobias Haslinger, all in Vienna. He published two volumes of songs privately in the last years of his life. Josef Hüttenbrenner wrote twice to C.F. Peters in Leipzig, the famous publishing firm. They replied they had to publish the work of 'their friends' Spohr, Romberg, Hummel – where are they now? – and had 'no time for an unknown composer'. Schubert read the letter. He did not bother to reply.

But on 12 August 1826 – the day he wrote to Breitkopf & Härtel – he sent a letter to another Leipzig publisher, Heinrich Albert Probst, offering three pieces at eighty gulden each. Probst replied that the price was too high. He met Schubert early in 1827 in Vienna and asked for works that were 'not too difficult to grasp'. Schubert offered him a volume of songs or piano pieces, apparently 'not too difficult', asking for sixty gulden. Probst accepted on the condition that he could also publish the Piano Trio Op. 100. Schubert reluctantly agreed because he wanted 'to make a start', though the trio was 'six times as much work'. On 2 October 1828 Schubert offered Probst his last three piano sonatas, the String Quintet, and the Heine songs. They are among his greatest works. Schubert died six weeks later, not knowing that Probst had turned down the manuscripts.

His dealings with the famous firm of B. Schott's Sons, who had published Beethoven's last quartets and the *Missa Solemnis*, were equally discouraging. They wrote to him saying they were always interested 'in piano works or songs'. Schubert hopefully offered them almost a hundred works, among them the magnificent String Quartet in D minor (*Der Tod und das Mädchen*), the great Quartet in G major, three operas and the Mass in A flat. He also mentioned his Gastein-Gmunden Symphony, 'in order to acquaint you with my striving for the highest in art'. Schott asked for some of the offered works but not for the string quartets and some songs. Nor, unfortunately, did he ask for the Gastein-Gmunden Symphony, of which nothing is known.

Schubert had learned his lesson and became more careful. He sent Schott only copies of the Piano Trio in E flat major, the Impromptus, and the male voice chorus *Mondenschein*. Schott turned down the great trio ('too long') but meanwhile Schubert had sold it to Probst. On 2 October 1828 Schubert asked Schott what had happened to the other things he had submitted. He never found out. The *Mondenschein* chorus was published in 1830, two years after his death, and the Impromptus in 1838 – but by Diabelli, not by Schott. The music publishers have no reason to be proud about Franz Schubert.

In 1826 Hans Georg Nägeli in Zürich approached Schubert through Karl Czerny, the noted pianist, asking for a piano sonata that would be included in a new volume of collected pieces. Schubert asked for an advance of 120 florins, but Nägeli never replied. On 25 July 1827 Schubert wrote to his parents, 'If only one could do honest business with these art-dealers! But the State, in its wisdom and benevolence, has seen to it that the artist shall remain for all time the slave of every miserable pedlar.' Not much has changed since then.

Schubert's income was not as low as is sometimes assumed but it was never adequate. But how much does one pay a genius? Schubert was paid in florins. It is almost impossible to express the value of his earnings in today's inflated currencies, it can be done only relatively. In the last two years of his life Schubert earned 1090 and 1310 florins respectively. With fees for commissioned liturgical works, performance fees, teaching fees, and presents from friends and admirers, he may have made about 1500 florins a year, worth approximately £150 at contemporary rates. By comparison it has been suggested that when Thomas Carlyle set up house in London in 1834 with his wife his annual income was £150.

Thus the legend of Schubert 'the penniless genius' is just another Schubert legend. Schwind tells us that Schubert liked 'pheasants and punch'. When he had money to spend, he spent it. Bauernfeld later wrote, 'We alternated between want and plenty. Among the three of us it was Schubert who played the part of a Croesus and who, off and on, would be rolling in money.' Not often though. Bauernfeld remembers another occasion when he went to the coffeehouse near the Kärntnertor and ordered coffee and half a dozen *Kipfel*. It was already afternoon, he had no money and had eaten nothing all day long. Then Schubert appeared, just as penniless, and also ordered coffee and a few *Kipfel*. Both were unable to pay and told the waiter to put it on the bill. 'It was a time of utter want for both of us,' remembers Bauernfeld.

Though Schubert sometimes had a little money he never had real security. In this respect his father had been right after all about earning one's life as a composer. Only the opera house or the Church or possibly a rich, aristocratic patron might have given him that, and Schubert had none.

Schubert was not as restless as Beethoven who, according to O. E. Deutsch, lived in forty-four different places. By comparison Gluck and Haydn had their own houses in Vienna, but Mozart had eighteen different homes.

Schubert stayed in seventeen different places during his short life. He first lived with his family at Himmelpfortgrund and in Säulengasse and for some time at the Rossau School House where his father was the principal. After

Grillparzer's living
room.

staying with Spaun at Professor Watteroth's house in Landstrasse he lived
with Mayrhofer, in 1818, in Wipplingerstrasse 2. Three years later he lived
alone for the first time, at the Theatiner Convent. He stayed with Schober
in Tuchlauben, and in 1822 moved to Göttweigerhof (now Spiegelgasse 9).
Nearby was Grillparzer's room, now a museum, a typical Biedermeier flat
with a piano on which Schubert may have played when visiting Grillparzer,
who was a good pianist himself.

It was only a short walk to the Camesima House in Domgasse, another
'sanctified place' as Brahms later called it, where Mozart had composed *Le
Nozze di Figaro*. In 1825 Schubert rented a room at the Fruhwirthaus, near
Charles Church. Not far away was the Mondscheinhaus belonging to the
Schwind family. Forty-seven years later Brahms lived nearby at Karlsgasse
4. Musical Vienna remained a small, compact world. In 1827 Schubert
stayed at Blauer Igel in Tuchlauben with Schober. Early in September 1828
he moved into the new apartment of his brother Ferdinand in the Wieden
suburb 694 – and there he died.

The Immortal Lied

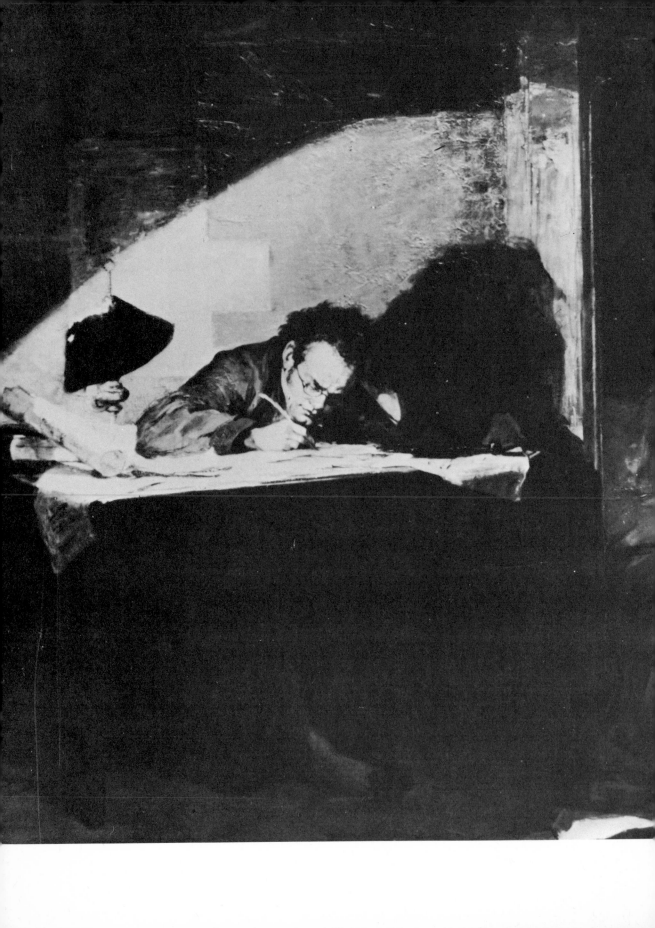

Most of the details of Schubert's short, uneventful life are known, and most of his works have been found and analysed. But we know more about Schubert the composer than about Schubert the man, who remains an enigma. Often Schubert reveals himself more in his music than in his day-to-day life. 'Where others keep a diary in which they record their momentary feelings, Schubert confided his passing moods to music paper; his soul, musical through and through, wrote notes where others resort to words,' wrote Schumann one year after Schubert's death.

Yet doubts remain. Schubert's work does not always reflect his feelings of the moment. From his friends' reminiscences we know that Schubert wrote melancholy music when he seemed relaxed, and often merry melodies when he was depressed. Thanks to O.E. Deutsch Schubert's life is more exactly documented than the career of many other composers. Deutsch sensed the complexity of Schubert, the immense abyss between 'Schwammerl', so deceivingly simple and gentle, and the composer with his passions and emotions who wrote the C major String Quintet or the Great C major Symphony. God knows what Sigmund Freud might have discovered if Schubert had lived a hundred years later. Freud lived in Berggasse, not far from many of the places where Schubert had stayed.

Musicologists often believe they can analyse a man out of his music. But musical notation is, at best, a blueprint. Schubert was more explicit in his scores than Haydn or Mozart. But he did not go as far as Richard Strauss or Gustav Mahler, who wrote as closely as possible how they wanted their music to be performed. We know how Schubert wanted his songs performed – he often spoke about it with his friends – but what about his orchestral masterpieces, such as the *Unfinished* Symphony or the Great C major Symphony which he never heard?

For a long time Schubert remained an artificial figure, a composite made up of clichés and legends. George Orwell once wrote that truisms really are true. Many Schubert clichés are not wrong. He was 'ein echtes Wiener

opposite Schubert at work.

Kind' – a genuine Viennese child. Born in one district of Vienna he spent most of his life in the city and died in another district. He seems to personify the *genius loci*; living in a musical environment he exuded music himself. As so many Viennese he loved life knowing it is short: Let us eat and drink; for tomorrow we die. It is this side of Schubert that was commercially exploited. Schubert, the awkward, lovable hero of *Dreimäderlhaus* (*Lilac Time*), of silly films, *Leise flehen meine Lieder*. But where is the *genius loci* when Schubert wrote *Heidenröslein* artfully creating a genuine folk song? Twelve years later he wrote another art song, 'Am Brunnen vor dem Tore' (*Der Lindenbaum* from *Winterreise*) that has become a folk song through the process of repetition – a song that is loved and sung so much that its composer is forgotten. But when one studies *Der Lindenbaum*, with its prelude and conclusion, the sensitive accompaniment, the use of the minor key for one verse, the wonderful *Lied* is pure art.

Nothing is simple about Schubert though it often seems so. In 1823 when he was sick and miserable, lying at the hospital, feeling low and depressed, he wrote a large part of the song cycle *Die schöne Müllerin*, one of his masterworks, often joyful and happy.

Having made the break with his family life and his past Schubert enjoyed his new freedom. But he was serious about it and really tried to learn his art. The hours spent in coffeehouses and wine gardens with his friends were not wasted; he was always listening, always learning. Occasionally he wrote some second-rate music. Brahms later said that Schubert was 'exercising his pen'. Lachner remembered a day in 1826 when he visited Schubert at the Fruhwirthaus.

He was not in the mood for work and glad of the distraction. He said 'Come, let's have some coffee', and fetched an old coffee mill, 'his most precious possession' as he called it, put in the beans and began to grind. Suddenly he called out, 'I've got it, you rusty little contraption!' and threw the grinder into a corner. He said 'A coffee mill like this is a wonderful thing. Melodies and themes just come flying in. You see it's this ra-ra-ra, that's what it is!... One sometimes searches for days for an idea which the little machine finds in a second. Listen!'

Schubert began to sing. Lachner later claimed he heard the themes of the String Quartet in D minor. Lachner noted them down quickly and then they gathered the spilled beans and the grinder, and eventually had their coffee. Lachner is not an absolutely reliable source though and he ends the anecdote with the statement that 'Schubert's mastery in preparing good strong Viennese coffee was not inferior to his art of composition'. But the point is that Schubert seems to have had his inspiration any time, anywhere.

His 'light touch' is deceiving. Schubert worked hard; he would pay much attention to the expression of a poem, he would often sing a new *Lied* for himself by way of trying it out. The impression conveyed by the reminiscences of his friends, that he led a carefree, easy-going life, is refuted by the catalogue of his works. Even a human being obviously loved by the gods, as Schubert was, had to work hard to create so much beauty in such a short time.

Bogner's Coffeehouse.

Schubert had the schoolmaster's habit of putting down the date of a finished work on each manuscript. The enormous research work done by O.E. Deutsch and others proves that Schubert did not spend so much of his time drinking and singing. Spaun claims that the references to Schubert's love of wine are exaggerated, that Schubert was temperate by nature, and besides was forced to remain so by the precarious state of his finances.

For many years I used to take supper with him at an inn and was frequently with him in convivial company, and never once did Schubert have too much of the good things in life. In summer time, on hot days, he liked going for long walks in the evening, not on account of the wine but because he was a lover of beautiful landscape … When one considers that he composed every day from early morning until two o'clock in the afternoon, at white heat and to the point of exhaustion, one will understand that he might enjoy a glass of wine or beer.

The manuscript of 'Klärchen's Song'.

Every *Lied* is a song but not every song is a *Lied*. People have sung throughout

the ages. Spiritual and secular songs go back to the seventh century but singing as an expression of human emotion is as old as mankind. The relationship between words and sounds was first resolved musically, with emphasis on the music; the vocal part was incorporated in the musical structure. Later the words became more important and the music was used mainly to accompany them. All this is demonstrated in the development of opera, oratorio and cantata. The classic era expressed the power of music which was at best absolute music. Then the romantic era, an era of poetry, turned people's attention towards poems set to music. Max Friedländer, in *Das deutsche Lied im 18 Jahrhundert*, proves that songs existed long before the romantic era. Schulz, Reichardt, Zelter and Zumsteeg wrote songs though most of them are now forgotten.

It is wrong to call Schubert 'Father of the Song'. But he alone created the modern German *Lied* that is now considered a musical species of its own, neither a 'song' nor a 'chanson'. Schubert probably experimented with the *Lied* as a young boy; he wrote his first masterpiece *Gretchen am Spinnrade* in 1814, when he was seventeen. Fourteen years later he wrote his last fourteen songs, published posthumously as *Schwanengesang* (Swan Song). Within this incredibly short space of time Schubert developed the *Lied* from beginning to perfection. It was a rough path – not all of the 600 and more songs he wrote are masterpieces – but Schubert's greatest *Lieder* remain unsurpassed though Schumann and Brahms come close to him occasionally.

The manuscript of 'Idens Nachtgesang' with words by Rosegarten. This was written in 1815, Schubert's most prolific year.

overleaf Schubert accompanies singing on the piano.

99

At first, instinctively and later consciously, Schubert created the ideal balance between poetry and music. He was the first composer to make harmony and the accompaniment as important as the melody and the words of the poem. It has been said that in Schubert's hands all poetry became music. He did not accept the supremacy of poetry, as so many song writers before him. He had good taste and great respect for fine poetry – his favourite poet, Goethe, wrote some of the finest German poetry – but he could not have written to his father, as Mozart did, that poetry must be 'the obedient daughter of music'.

Schubert sensed the ideal union of words and sounds, of voice and accompaniment. In his greatest songs the accompaniment is neither a mere harmonic help, as in the songs of the older song writers, nor is it a sort of symphony, with the vocal part as a mere voice among other orchestral voices, as in the songs of Mahler and Schönberg. In Schubert's masterpieces the accompaniment acts like the orchestra in the masterpieces of Mozart, Verdi or Wagner. The mood, the psychology, the enormous substance of the subconscious is in the accompaniment, the 'orchestra', though words and melodies are in the voice. In Mozart's *Figaro*, Verdi's *Otello*, Wagner's *Ring*, the singers may sing conscious lies but the truth is always there, in the orchestra.

(The accompaniment to Schubert's *Lieder* is often difficult and demands a musically and technically mature pianist who has a feeling for the spirit of Schubert. The best singers always try to get the best available pianists for their Schubert recitals. They consider the pianist a partner of equal status rather than a mere 'accompanist'. Schubert himself, a good though not an outstanding pianist, had definite ideas about the accompaniment of his songs. Several well-known concert pianists have been happy to play the accompaniments to the *Lieder*. Lotte Lehmann was often accompanied by Bruno Walter at the piano, Elisabeth Schumann by Karl Alwin and the formidable Gerald Moore, Hans Hotter by Moore and Michael Raucheisen. Artur Schnabel accompanied his wife, the alto Therese Behr-Schnabel, and in 1976 Vladimir Horowitz accompanied Fischer-Dieskau in Carnegie Hall.)

Schubert was a born melodist who wrote poetry in tones but had no sense of the lyrical drama. It was one of his great regrets that he never succeeded in writing a successful opera; his operas and operatic fragments contain gems of fine music but are dramatically ineffective. His finest melodies are so great though, musically and emotionally, that they can be sung without accompaniment and completely express the idea of the song. 'Schubert,' wrote Paul Henry Lang, 'was able to project the idea, that is the purely musical, through the image of the idea, the poem.' He was able to deeply penetrate into the poet's mind so that his musical version of the poem often expresses shades that even the poet was not able to say.

Much has been written about Goethe's arrogant treatment of Schubert. Even Goethe's admirers admit, reluctantly, that he was not knowledgeable about music. After a visit to the eighty-year-old Goethe in Weimar young Felix Mendelssohn wrote to his parents:

Schubert sent Goethe some musical settings of his poems but these were never acknowledged.

... Goethe is so friendly and affectionate with me that I do not know how to thank him or how I deserve it. In the morning I must play the piano for him for about an hour ... He would have none of Beethoven. But I told him I could not help that, and thereupon played for him the first movement of the Symphony in C minor. This affected him strangely. At first he said, 'But it does not move at all, it merely astounds, it is grandiose', and went on, growling to himself, until after a long time he began again, 'That is very great, quite mad, one is almost afraid the house will collapse. And imagine when they are all playing this together.'

This seems to have been the first time Goethe had heard the first movement of Beethoven's Fifth Symphony, a work that had been in the repertoire of the leading European orchestras for over twenty years! Yet this is not the explanation for his attitude in April 1816 when Spaun sent to Goethe sixteen handwritten, as yet unpublished, Schubert *Lieder* set to Goethe's poems. Among them were *Erlkönig*, *Gretchen am Spinnrade*, *Heidenröslein*. Spaun enclosed a somewhat stilted, subservient letter that may have aroused Goethe's dislike. It was never acknowledged and the package of *Lieder* was returned to Spaun. Perhaps Goethe never even opened it. He received many appeals for help and recommendations every day. But nine years later, in early June 1825, Schubert himself sent to Goethe three recently published Goethe songs – *An Schwager Kronos*, *An Mignon*, and *Ganymed*, with a letter:

Your Excellency,
If by the dedication of this setting of your poems I could succeed in recording my unlimited veneration for Your Excellency, and perhaps in gaining some attention for my humble self, I would praise the favourable outcome of this wish as the happiest event of my life.

With the greatest respect,
Your humble, devoted servant,
Franz Schubert

Schubert usually wrote beautiful, natural letters, reflecting the pleasant side of his personality. 'Only when writing to men of exalted standing (*grosse Herren*) or to those whom he modestly considered much greater than himself, Schubert lost his free style,' writes O. E. Deutsch. Max Friedländer who first published Schubert's letter to Goethe wrote, 'It is too bad that Schubert whose letters to his friends often have fortunate, unconscious poetic expressions, was always very clumsy in his official writings.'

Goethe noted the receipt of the letter in his dairy, 'Package from Schubert in Vienna, compositions of my *Lieder*.' Goethe never answered the letter and Schubert felt humiliated. Goethe's attitude has been discussed by generations of biographers. Some suggest it was more than mere lack of understanding. Goethe may have been many things to many men but he was no fool. These were his poems and he had heard of Schubert. Could he have sensed, with the poet's instinctive knowledge, that Schubert's settings had turned his, Goethe's, poetry into Schubert's *Lieder*? That Schubert might have expressed his, Goethe's poetry in greater depth than he had done it with his words? He did not seem to mind when his friends Reichardt and Zelter set his poems to music. He knew that his verse would safely dominate their

Schubert's setting of Goethe's *Prometheus*.

melodies. In his later years, when discussing the nature of genius, Goethe would mention Mozart who seemed to him 'the human incarnation of the divine force of creation'. However Goethe did not think of Mozart as a pure musician, he was interested in the musical-dramatist genius of Mozart. He wrote to Schiller, 'The hopes you placed in opera you would find fulfilled to a high degree in the recent *Don Juan (Don Giovanni)*.'

Goethe may also have been upset by Schubert's taking some liberties with the poet's words. Schubert's *Gretchen am Spinnrade* is emotionally stronger than Goethe's somewhat different poem; the universal language of music is more powerful than any written poetry. On a different level Verdi's *Otello* is more exciting than Shakespeare's *Othello*. It is perhaps tragic that the poet and the composer of *Heidenröslein* never met. But they were worlds apart. In 1825, when Schubert wrote his letter, he was insecure and depressed, twenty-eight and had three more years to live. Goethe, famous, secure, often disdainful, was seventy-six and had seven more years left.

An argument exists among Schubert's biographers, depending on where they come from, as to how much of Schubert's work is typically Viennese. How much of it is born out of the ambience of Vienna, which is a musical fact not fiction? 'All depth and insight, the warmth and grace of his feelings, his easy-goingness and sometimes his shallowness (*Flachheit*) are in his *Lieder*,' the Viennese critic Ludwig Speidel wrote in 1884. Not only in his songs. Schubert's finest music is that inimitable blend of lightheartedness and melancholy that is a very Viennese mixture.

From Munich Alfred Einstein asks:

What is there Viennese in that field, in which he is at his greatest? There Schubert is much too independent to be contained by purely regional boundaries ... His songs did not have their roots in Vienna ... but in Svabia or North Germany, and, from a spiritual or poetical standpoint, in the general German renaissance. And what is there Viennese in his instrumental works? Is there anything Viennese in the last three quartets, the String Quintet, the two Piano Trios or the Piano Sonatas?

Hans Gal, born near Vienna and trained there, feels there is an anti-Vienna language barrier among Schubert's biographers.

... those pieces in which the music not only suggests the local background, but breaks spontaneously into the vernacular, such as the *Trout* Quintet, the two Piano Trios and the Piano Sonata in D major, have over and over aroused annoyance and disdainful rejection ... With Schubert deplorable distortions still occur. They concern peculiarities of rhythm and phrasing too subtle to be expressed in the written notes, which can never be more than an appreciation. Schubert's phrase cannot stand the restriction of a stiff collar ...

A meaningless argument but it is repeated time and again. Some biographers believe that 'biographically' Schubert is a Moravian or Silesian composer: his father came from Neudorf near Mährisch-Schönberg in Moravia, his mother from Zuckmantel in Austria's Silesia. Both later came to Vienna which attracted people in earlier centuries as New York attracts them in the twentieth century. The whole thing is ridiculous, of course. Is Mozart partly German because his father came from Augsburg? In the case of Beethoven, the problem is even more complex. The truth is that Mozart, Beethoven and Schubert have long belonged to the world at large.

Schubert is certainly the most Viennese among the great composers. Of all great people who came to Vienna and created music there he and the Johann Strauss dynasty with Joseph Lanner are the only genuine Viennese. Later, much later, they were joined by Arnold Schönberg and Alban Berg. Some works of Schubert express the *genius loci* more strongly than others. At the Höldrichsmühle in suburban Hinterbrühl is the linden tree – more exactly its trunk which is all that remains – that is said to have inspired Schubert to compose *Der Lindenbaum*. That could be true, or it could be another *se non è vero, è ben trovato*. 'In summer time he loved to walk in the Wienerwald,' writes Joseph Spaun. 'On a nice evening he might forget that he had been invited to an elegant town house and there might be trouble, which didn't worry him much.' Brahms, who often went to the Höldrichsmühle, once said, 'A good thing that Schubert research has not yet been able to establish it. How many memorial tablets would have to be set up in Vienna! With every step we are treading on classical soil!' Brahms who came from Northern Germany wrote some of his finest music in Vienna.

Schubert loved Vienna and was unhappy during his short absences from the city. He writes so in his letters. But as he grew, in spite of his limitations, and began writing great music, he stopped being a local Viennese composer and became a lonely genius. He shares this duplicity with other composers of the various Viennese schools. Mozart's *Die Zauberflöte* is often typically Viennese owing to Schikaneder's libretto, but the opera's great moments, the Pamina-Papageno duet 'Bei Männern welche Liebe fühlen' or Tamino's 'Dies Bildnis is bezaubernd schön' are not Viennese but timeless, unrelated, absolute. *Figaro* and *Don Giovanni* are neither Italian or Viennese but magnificent Mozart. And perhaps some Viennese may admit that Beethoven's *Pastoral* Symphony is not Viennese, though the place exists where the composer was inspired to write *Szene am Bach*.

Great music knows no boundaries. Great artists are inspired everywhere and must not be tied down to nationality or region. Beethoven's last quartets, composed in Vienna, are absolute music. Even the important national composers rise above the restriction in their finest works. In such moments Smetana and Dvořák are no longer Czechs, Mussorgsky and Rimsky-Korsakov are no longer Russians, and what is French in the masterpieces of Debussy and Ravel? Even Johann Strauss, in his greatest waltzes such as *The Emperor Waltz*, is not a Viennese composer but a great composer. The local label is always somewhat suspect. *Der Rosenkavalier* is known as a Viennese opera because of Hofmannsthal's libretto and the waltzes by Richard Strauss. They tried to write a 'comedy for music', hoping to come close to the ideal of *Le Nozze di Figaro*. What they actually created is an amusing Viennese comedy with music.

Vienna from the 'Spinnerin Kreutz'.

The piano in Schubert's study.

What is really astonishing about Schubert is that, although he never wanted to leave Vienna and never left Austria, his genius crossed the boundaries of nationality in a similar fashion to Haydn, Mozart, and Beethoven who, on the contrary, all travelled a great deal. Sometimes to the casual listener Schubert may sound like Mozart. On the other hand there are moments when Mozart sounds almost like Schubert, who was not even born when Mozart died. The musical scale – both in the classical sense and in the meaning of Schönberg's twelve semitones – has only a limited number of sounds, and there is always a chance of two similar sounding melodies. Sometimes a composer uses a phrase invented by an earlier one – not to 'steal' it but to show his devotion and gratitude. It is said that the *Unfinished* Symphony and the String Quintet 'could have been written' by Beethoven. But similarly some phrases and melodies in Beethoven's works could have been composed by Schubert. Schubert's *Lied, Hagars Klage*, consciously follows the earlier setting of Johann Rudolf Zumsteeg. Perhaps the young man wanted to prove to himself he could do it better. When Eusebius Mandyczewski edited the *Lieder* in the Complete Edition of Schubert's Works he logically added Zumsteeg's version, and two others, to show the 'similarity'. It is quite obvious that Schubert's setting is the best.

And thus the pointless argument remains undecided. Both sides are right or both are wrong. There is the Viennese influence in everything Schubert wrote. He was Viennese and he wrote as he felt. But his masterpieces are not Viennese in the vernacular sense; they are great. Sometimes there is a waltzlike Viennese melody in his late, timeless masterpieces such as the Scherzo in the G major Quartet, that sounds as though played by a 'Schrammel' ensemble – violin, clarinet, guitar – at a Viennese Heuriger tavern. And he used some 'local idiom' in his Piano Sonata in D major, with its delightful Scherzo and the fine Finale that was later pilfered by the manufacturers of *Lilac Time*.

The Viennese influence is strong in Schubert's letters. He often employs local dialect when discussing routine matters. This often happens in Vienna today, where the inhabitants speak both their dialect and a somewhat stilted *Hochdeutsch*. Schubert and his friends probably spoke in the various shades of Viennese dialects. The legend of Schubert's Great C major Symphony may have been unwittingly started by Robert Schumann who wrote:

... this Vienna, with its St Stephen's Spire, its lovely women, its public pageantry ... this Vienna, with all its memories of the greatest German masters, must be fruitful ground for the musician's fancy. Often as I gazed at it from the mountain heights I used to imagine how Beethoven's eyes must constantly have wandered restlessly towards that distant range of the Alps. How Mozart, lost in thought, must often have followed the course of the Danube ... how Papa Haydn must many a time have contemplated St Stephen's ... The sights stir within us chords which would otherwise never have sounded. Schubert's symphony, with the clear romantic spirit that quickens it, brings the city more vividly before my eyes today than ever before, and makes me understand once again how it is that such works come to be born in surroundings like these ...

That is the stuff of which legends are created.

Some people claim that Schubert had doubtful literary taste because he often used second-rate poetry. The fact is that he turned such second-rate poetry into first-class *Lieder*, which are so beautiful that we are no longer aware of the quality of the poetry. Schubert was not the only composer who turned inferior poems into superior songs; Schumann, Brahms and Hugo Wolf also did so. There must be something even in an inferior poem – inferior in the literary sense – that strikes the composer's imagination and an inner chord in his soul. No one would recite Georg Philipp Schmidt's poem *Der Wanderer* if Schubert had not turned it into one of his masterpieces. Some of his lyricists – Jacobi, Kosegarten, Pyrker, Fellinger, Roos – are widely unknown. Both 'Sah ein Knab' ein Röslein stehn' and 'Das Wandern ist des Müllers Lust' have become folk songs. But *Heidenröslein* was written by Goethe and the other text by Wilhelm Müller from Dessau, a patriotic poet during the Napoleonic wars whose work has been called sentimental, lachrymose, full of *Weltschmerz*, sometimes close to *Kitsch*. Ludwig Rellstab, who shares with Heinrich Heine the distinction of having written some poems which Schubert composed in his last year in *Swan Song*, would now be forgotten without Schubert's music.

Schubert, the musical lyricist, created with his heart and with his mind; probably the heart came first. He was always looking for a poem that would inspire him, and when a line, a rhyme, an image caught his imagination, he would set down the poem to music. He had the mysterious ability of penetrating into the soul of any poet. He wrote *Heidenröslein* on that blessed 19 August 1815 when he was eighteen years old. He felt it was good and never revised it. But on the same day he also wrote some other songs that are perhaps among his 'writing exercises'. Proof again that the mystery of creation cannot be analysed. When he began writing the *Winterreise* songs in February 1827 he was tormented by terrible headaches and was depressed by the increasing awareness of his 'commercial' failure. Earlier he told Bauernfeld, 'I can already see you as a *Hofrat* and famous author of comedies. But what will become of me, the poor *Musikant*? When I get old, I'll have to sneak up to doors, like Goethe's harpist, begging for bread.'

Schubert worked hard on the *Winterreise Lieder* but had to give them away, pressed by sickness and the need for some money. Lachner took the first songs, among them *Der Lindenbaum*, to the music publisher Haslinger. He had been told to bring back some money so Schubert could pay for some food and the doctor. Lachner later wrote, 'The publisher immediately realized the situation and paid – one florin for each *Lied*.' But Lachner's memory was not very good: Tobias Haslinger announced publication of the first twelve *Lieder* of *Winterreise* only on 14 January 1828. Schubert read proofs of the last songs of the cycle on his death bed. They were published several weeks after he died.

At a time when most people, sick and depressed, retire into silence and despair, Schubert's melodic invention was at its zenith. In *Winterreise* he became a great tone poet. The cycle contains allusions to his despair, his overwhelming melancholy, 'Wie weit noch bis zum Grabe' (how far still to my grave?) or when he sings about *Gefrorene Tränen* (Frozen Tears). And suddenly there is a ray of hope, as in *Die Post* with its moments of exuberant joy.

The dark emotions of *Winterreise* have caused many people who love Schubert to stay away from the cycle. They are oppressed by the overwhelming sense of despair. Musically *Winterreise* is a phenomenon. For the first time Schubert gives his songs a large, almost instrumental form, revealing his very soul, the complete truth with its many psychological complications. The piano accompaniment creates the mood while the voice presents the changing images – a perfect blend.

Perhaps only an artist able to sing Schubert's *Lieder* cycles so that they express almost everything Schubert was trying to say is able to understand the complexity of his genius. Analysis is one thing, but recreating the emotional wealth of Schubert with the human voice – for which he wrote the music – is another. Ideally the singer should also be a writer, trying to explain why he interprets the songs in a certain way. An almost impossible combination, but Dietrich Fischer-Dieskau comes close to it in his book *Auf den Spuren der Schubert Lieder* (On the Tracks of Schubert's Songs).

Fischer-Dieskau writes that for many years he hesitated to sing *Winterreise* in public. He asked himself whether 'such an intimate diary of the soul' should be offered to the public. Eventually he answered the question to himself the way Schubert might have answered it. Yes – if one makes no concession to a public that expects to be entertained, 'no concession to Austrian charm or lachrymal bliss'. Which makes a performance of *Winterreise* a monumental task, since the songs demand more than lyrical expression. They often reach dramatic climaxes.

Today though there is an audience for such suffering, for the lonely monologue of a tortured soul. But many people who love the songs of *Winterreise* admit that they would rather listen to a good recording in seclusion where they do not have to worry about having so suppress their feelings, or coming close to tears.

Modern copyright did not exist in Schubert's time. That a musical idea, a melody, a poem should belong to its creator would have caused astonishment. Today people are punished for stealing a pair of stockings in a department store but they often get away with stealing somebody else's idea. Only in a few countries are authors paid for the use of their works in public libraries. The latest methods of reproduction make it almost impossible to prevent the piracy of words and sounds. Intellectual property is not as well protected as material property.

When Schubert liked a poem he would set it to music. It would never have occurred to him to ask for permission. Often he did not know the poet personally. He and his friends were great readers. They 'discovered' not only Goethe and Schiller but A.W. and Friedrich von Schlegel, Rückert, Platen, Uhland, Novalis, and Heine whose poetry was read in Schober's house in January 1828. Heinrich Heine's *Reisebilder* had been published in 1826. Schubert found six poems in *Die Heimkehr*, the opening of *Reisebilder*, and set them to music for his last *Lieder*, later published as *Schwanengesang*. He even wrote the titles which Heine had not done. On 2 October 1828, six weeks before his death, Schubert wrote to two publishers, Schott in Mainz and Probst in Leipzig, 'I have set several *Lieder* by Heine from Hamburg which were appreciated here very highly ...'

Heine was later curious about what his poems might have been like after Schubert had turned them into *Lieder*. Most poets – with the exception of Goethe, the Olympian – were pleased to have their poems set by Schubert and some sensed, quite correctly, that he had given their work a new dimension. We know this from the Viennese poets whose work Schubert used – Mayrhofer, Seidel, Castelli, Grillparzer – and from the comments of his friends.

But the lack of adequate copyright laws worked both ways. Schubert took whatever he liked. And his own music was often expropriated. There is no evidence that he cared; he knew he could always write another melody. One of Schubert's popular dance tunes is the *Trauerwalzer* (Sorrow Waltz) Op. 9 No. 2, that was published in 1821 with thirty-five other dance tunes. Anselm Hüttenbrenner owned a copy into which Schubert wrote his dedication, 'Written for my coffee, wine and punch companion Anselm Hüttenbrenner, world-famous composer. Vienna, 14th March in the year of our Lord 1818, in his very own most exalted abode, for 30 florins.'

After Schubert's death the catchy tune was stolen and published anonymously in German, French and English editions. One Johann Pensel, a contemporary of Schubert's, wrote *Variations on the Popular Sorrow Waltz*. Karl Czerny, the pianist, wrote *Variations on a Favourite Viennese Waltz*. Later the tune was ascribed to Beethoven – by B. Schott's Sons in Mainz, Beethoven's publishers, who should and may have known the truth. Perhaps they thought the name Beethoven would sell more copies. Just in case the tune was renamed *Sehnsuchts-Walzer* (Longing Waltz).

The error was rectified only fifty years later in the Complete Edition of Schubert's Works. But that was not the end. The tune was appropriated

Heinrich Heine.

by the arrangers of *Dreimäderlhaus* and was sung, hummed and whistled all over the world. Not only books, melodies too have their fates.

Every era has only a few great singers, our memories notwithstanding, and among them there are very few *Lieder* singers, especially those able to sing Schubert. The roll call begins with the lucky ones, who were accompanied by Schubert at the piano and who sang his songs the way he wanted them sung: Johann Michael Vogl, Karl von Schönstein, Ludwig Tietze (who was often called an 'amateur' or 'dilettante' but did a lot for Schubert). After Schubert's death Julius Stockhausen, 'the Alsatian with the sonorous baritone voice', performed Schubert's cycles, *Die schöne Müllerin* and *Winterreise*, all over Europe. Brahms, who dedicated to him the *Magelone* songs, sometimes accompanied Stockhausen on the piano. Stockhausen had studied with the great Manuel Garcia and had a subtle understanding for the spirit of Schubert's *Lieder*. After he retired to Frankfurt he taught many young singers what he knew of Schubert.

Stockhausen was the first singer who dared arrange *Lieder* recitals; the *Lieder* were usually by Schubert. Gustav Walter, a noted tenor at the court opera, sang Schubert Lieder at the Bösendorfer Hall, and Stockhausen's pupil, Karl Scheidemantel the famous Bayreuth Amfortas, sang *Wanderer* and *Erlkönig*. These songs were also performed by the great Theodor Reichmann, who occasionally exaggerated Schubert's effects; at the end of *Erlkönig* he would not sing, but speak with a hollow voice the final words '...war tot'. Viktor Heim started to sing complete *Schubertiaden* at the Höldrichsmühle near Mödling, a suburb of Vienna, where according to tradition Schubert had written *Der Lindenbaum*. Hans Duhan, the great lyrical baritone with the velvety voice, was the first singer who recorded the song cycles of Schubert. I remember him well; he performed the rarely heard *Lieder*, *Heliopolis* and *Grenzen der Menschheit*. Two great stars of the Vienna Opera who often appeared with Duhan were Leo Slezak, the unforgotten tenor, and Richard Mayr, the original Ochs von Lerchenau. Both loved to perform the songs of Schubert. Lotte Lehmann, also a member of the Opera at that time, often sang Schubert *Lieder* accompanied by Bruno Walter. But most Schubert interpreters were men. 'Schubert offers much more to a man's voice than to the women who are better in the songs of Schumann and Brahms,' writes Fischer-Dieskau.

Among the artists of more recent times who have recreated for us the magic world of Schubert are Hans Hotter (who made beautiful recordings with Michael Raucheisen and Gerald Moore), Julius Patzak, Karl Schmitt-Walter (who performed *Winterreise* with Ferdinand Leitner), Richard

Tauber, Peter Anders, Fritz Wunderlich. Today many famous singers attempt Schubert and some have become outstanding interpreters – Anton Dermota, Christa Ludwig, Peter Pears, Hermann Prey, Peter Schreier, Dietrich Fischer-Dieskau, and others.

No two of them sing Schubert alike, but many of them sing Schubert beautifully. Schubert has created a whole world of melody and there are many ways leading into it.

6

'A Certain Attractive Star'

Franz Schubert

Den 10 Juli 1821

Schubert hated to leave Vienna, the only place where he felt at home, but in July 1818 he went to the estate of Count Johann Karl Esterházy in Zseliz, on the Gran River in Western Hungary, as domestic music teacher. Count Esterházy was not a close relation of Haydn's former musical patrons, Prince Paul Anton and Prince Nicholas Joseph Esterházy. Schubert was to give lessons to the Count's daughters. Karl Freiherr von Schönstein who met Schubert there – they became friends – remembered in 1857, 'The Count's two daughters were Marie, afterwards Countess Breunner, and Caroline, later the wife of Count Crenneville. Schubert's task was more of coaching than teaching. He had been recommended by the father of Caroline Unger who later became a famous singer.'

Schubert quite often wrote to Schober and the other friends, and to his brothers and sisters. At first everything seemed fairly well. 'I live and compose like a god,' he wrote but then he admitted, 'I live at least, otherwise I should have become a frustrated musician.' A few weeks later he wrote, 'Happy as I am and well as I feel and kind as the people are here, I still look forward, day in day out, to the moment when I can say, "To Vienna, to Vienna!"' He was very homesick. When letters from Schober, Mayrhofer, Spaun and Senn arrived he would exclaim with joy. As his employment was extended into the autumn he became miserable. He would not stay one moment longer than was absolutely necessary. 'Not a soul here has a feeling for true art, except the Countess occasionally, if I am not mistaken. So I am alone with my beloved, and have to hide her in my room, in my piano, and in my heart. Although this often makes me sad, it also helps to inspire me the more.'

Schubert's room was not in the castle but in the inspectorate where other employees lived; a music teacher was only a better sort of servant. But Schubert's sense of humour is obvious in his description of life in Zseliz, written on 8 September 1818 in a letter addressed to 'Dear Schober! Dear Spaun! Dear Mayrhofer! Dear Senn! Dear Streinsberg! Dear Wayss!':

opposite A portrait of Schubert in 1821 by Kupelwieser.

119

opposite The music-room
at Zseliz.

... (My room) is fairly quiet except for 40 geese which sometimes set up such a cackling that one cannot hear oneself speak. The people round me are all, without exception, very nice ... The steward fits his office perfectly, a man with an extraordinary insight into his pockets and moneybags. The doctor, who is really clever, ails like an old woman at the age of twenty-four. All very unnatural. The surgeon, who is my favourite, is a much-respected, old man of seventy-five, always bright and cheerful. God grant to each of us such a happy old age. The magistrate is a very honest, decent sort of man. A companion of the Count, a cheerful old soul and an excellent musician, often keeps me company. The cook, the chambermaid, the housemaid, the governess, the butler etc., and the two grooms are all very nice. The cook is something of a rake, the chambermaid thirty years old, the housemaid very pretty and often my companion, the governess a good old thing, the butler my rival. The two grooms are more at home with horses than with human beings. The Count is rather rough; the Countess haughty but more refined; the two little girls are nice children. So far I have been spared the ordeal of dining with the family.

There are touches of Balzac and Dickens in Schubert's letter. He might have become a good writer had he not given his life to 'his beloved', his music. He deals with all the employees and only briefly, at the very end, with the members of the family. The reference to the 'very pretty' housemaid, 'often my companion', and to the butler's being 'my rival' has created speculation on a possible affair, and on the pretty housemaid's being the cause of the disease that had such a debilitating influence in Schubert's later years. But there is no proof and it may be part of the Schubert *mystique*. It is quite possible that Schubert became sick later in Vienna, around 1822.

In the autumn of 1818 he wrote, 'I now see that I am really lonely among them (the people around me), except for a couple of really nice girls. My longing for Vienna grows daily.' Some of his friends thought he might have fallen in love with the Esterházy girls, perhaps Caroline the younger one. Schönstein remembers, 'Caroline had the greatest regard for him and his talent but did not return his love. Once when she reproached Schubert in fun for having dedicated no composition to her, he replied, "What's the point? Everything is dedicated to you anyway."'

In May 1824 Schubert once more went to Zseliz as music teacher, and to write an opera and a symphony, as he told his friends. He wrote neither the opera nor the symphony but staying in the country was good for his health; he had not yet recovered from his sickness. In July he wrote to his brother Ferdinand, 'Admittedly it is no longer that happy time during which every object seems to us to be surrounded by the bright splendour of youth, but rather a time of fateful recognition of a miserable reality which I try as best as I can to beautify by my imagination.' Much can be read from these lines. At twenty-seven Schubert seems much older, with a heavy sense of resignation, as though he knew not much time remained. Later in this

letter he mentions 'a certain attractive star' in the castle and adds, 'We imagine that happiness is to be found in places where once we were happy, whereas it lies in ourselves and although I had an unpleasant disappointment and saw repeated here an experience I had before in Steyr. But I am now better able to find happiness and tranquillity within myself than I was then.'

Schubert is often shy and gentle in his letters and merely indicates matters. The 'unpleasant disappointment' may have been caused by someone who told him he was 'only' the music teacher, though during his second visit to Zseliz he had his room at the castle. The 'attractive star' probably was

The Esterhazy estate at Zseliz.

Countess Caroline, and Schubert was doubtless aware of the enormous social distance between them. Earlier he wrote to Schober:

... Here I am, all alone, in the depths of Hungary, where I have unfortunately allowed myself to be lured for a second time, without having a single person with whom I could exchange an intelligent word. Since the time when you left I have hardly written any songs but have worked at various instrumental things. Heaven alone knows what is going to happen to my operas. Although I have been in good health again for the last five months the absence of you and Kupel (Kupelwieser) often lowers my spirits, and my days are sometimes very miserable ...

Caroline Esterhazy.

The 'various instrumental things' included two piano duets, perhaps written for his pupils. They are among Schubert's important piano compositions: the Duo in C major and the *Divertissement à l'Hongroise*. Liszt later arranged it for piano solo and also for full orchestra. Schubert never wrote a piano concerto. He had come to dislike the virtuoso technique of the solo part that was demanded after Beethoven. For Schubert the piano remained an intimate instrument rather than a virtuoso one. He had no exaggerated opinion of his own piano playing. On 25 (or 28) July 1825 he wrote to his father and stepmother from Steyr saying he had performed the Variations from his A minor Sonata Op. 42 'alone and not without being lucky, as some people assured me that the keys under my fingers had become singing voices. If this is true, I am very pleased, since I cannot stand the damnable thumping (*Hacken*) which is peculiar even to excellent pianists and which pleases neither the ear nor the mind.'

Schönstein remembers that in September 1824 Schubert composed in Zseliz the four-part poem *Gebet* (Prayer) by Friedrich Freiherr de la Motte Fouqué for a quartet of mixed voices. It was published ten years after his death by Diabelli. 'The Countess had asked him to set the poem. He smiled inwardly, as he usually did when something appealed to him, took the book and retired to compose. In the evening of the same day we were already rehearsing the finished song, with Schubert at the piano. He had produced it in barely ten hours. It certainly seems incredible, but it is nevertheless true.'

Schönstein later became one of the best interpreters of Schubert's *Lieder*. Schubert accompanied Schönstein to Vienna in October. He dedicated to him his song cycle *Die schöne Müllerin*. Schubert was happy, for a change. In 1818 he had been paid 300 florins for four months in Zseliz – seventy-five florins a month. This time he had earned 100 florins a month and had 500 florins, a small fortune. And, best of all, he was back in his beloved Vienna.

Vienna during the first fifteen years after the Congress – the last years in Schubert's life – was outwardly, deceivingly calm. But Metternich's and Sedlnitzky's spies and informers were around. The old aristocratic families were still there but less in evidence than the socially prominent new noblemen, the bankers, merchants, manufacturers. They and their wives were interested in 'culture'. Culture was a status symbol and culture often meant music. And there were a few Kaiser-Koniglich (imperial-royal) officials, such as *Hofrat* Grillparzer, and university professors (Watteroth), often surrounded by students who did not like the new order. Many university

The Congress of Vienna, 1815.

students fought on the barricades during the Revolution of 1848 that drove out Metternich. But that was still the future. For the time being there was a widespread malaise that also affected Schubert and his friends.

Music was a safe retreat. Metternich and Gentz, who hated the 'pestilential poison' of political journalism, could not prohibit or even restrict music which was listened to and loved by all classes of the population. Schubert was feted at the Sonnleithners, the Geymüllers and in a few other wealthy homes. But he never really tried to gain an aristocratic patron, and when he found one, such as Karl Freiherr von Schönstein, the patron became another Schubertian, a friend and propagator of Schubert's songs.

The old values disappeared fast. Ten years before Schubert was born Emperor Joseph II could not help taking notice – not always benevolently – of Mozart who had created *Le Nozze di Figaro* and *Don Giovanni*. Around 1797, when Schubert was born, the aristocratic sponsors who had shown

Morgen Mittwoch den 7. März 1821
wird
in dem k. k. Hoftheater nächst dem Kärnthnerthore
mit hoher Bewilligung,

eine große musikalische Akademie

mit Declamation und Gemählde = Darstellungen
verbunden, gegeben werden.
Die einzelnen Gegenstände sind folgende:

Erste Abtheilung:

1. Die Ouverture des Schauspiels: Die Templer auf Cypern.
2. Ein Tableau: Die von Abraham verstoßene Hagar, nach Vandyck, dargestellt von Dlle. Hruschka, k. k. Hofschauspielerinn, Mad. Vogl, k. k. Hofopernstinn, Hrn. Vogl, k. k. Hofopernsten, Dlle. Kraft d. ält., Dlle. Pichler, Herren Pfeiffer, Segatta, Rossi und anderen Mitgliedern des Balletcorps.
3. Eine Arie von Mozart, gesungen von Dlle Wilh. Schröder.
4. Der erste Satz des zweyten Violinconcertes von L. Spohr, gespielt von Hrn. Leon de St. Lubin, dermaligem Schüler des Hrn. Professors der Violine, Joseph Böhm.
5. Der kleine Gernegroß, ein Gedicht von Langbein, vorgetragen von Mad. Wilhelmine Korn, k. k. Hofschauspielerinn.
6. Das Dörfchen, ein Gedicht von Bürger, für zwey Tenor = und zwey Baßstimmen gesetzt von Hrn Franz Schubert, vorgetragen von den Herren Götz und Barth, in Diensten Sr. Durchlaucht des regierenden Herrn Fürsten von Schwarzenberg, und den Herren Nejebse und Umlauf.
7. Variationen für das Pianoforte, componirt von Hrn. Hugo Worzizek, auf zwey Instrumenten gespielt von den zwey Dlles Schadt.
8. Ein Tableau: Sokrates vor seinen Richtern, nach Füger, dargestellt von dem Hrn. Richinger Vater und Sohn, Reiperger d. ält., Destefani, Rossi, Jos Kohlnberg, Pfeiffer, Wiesenbeck, Segatta und anderen Mitgliedern des Balletcorps.

Zweyte Abtheilung:

9. Die Ouverture der Oper die Zauberglocke (la Clochette), von Boieldieu.
10. Eine Arie von Mozart: Da ich einsam vor dir stehe, gesungen von Dlle. Unger, k. k. Hofopernstinn.
11. Die Gräfinn Spastara im Erdbeben von Messina, 1785, ein Gedicht, vorgetragen von Mad. Sophie Schröder, k. k. Hofschauspielerinn.
12. Der Erlkönig, Gedicht von Göthe, in Musik gesetzt von Franz Schubert, vorgetragen von Hrn. Vogl, k. k. Hofopernsten, auf dem Pianoforte begleitet von Hrn. Anselm Hüttenbrenner.
13. Adagio und Rondo für das Violoncell von Bernhard Romberg, gespielt von Hrn. Pechaczek.
14. Duett aus der Oper: Riccardo e Zoraide, von Rossini (Invan tu fingi, ingrata), gesungen von den Dlles. Schröder und Unger.
15. Der Gesang der Geister über den Wassern, Gedicht von Göthe, für vier Tenor = und vier Baßstimmen gesetzt von Hrn Franz Schubert, vorgetragen von den Herren Götz, Barth, Nejebse, Umlauf, Weinkopf, Frühwald und zwey Chorsängern, gespielt von Hrn. Pechaczek.
16. Ein Tableau: Aurora, nach Guido Reni, dargestellt von Hrn. Taglioni, erstem Tänzer der k. k. Hoftheater, und den Dlles. Neuwirth, Mayer, Krevaß, Kreiner, Wittwer, Eißele, Pichler, Kraft d. ält., Fanny Eßler und anderen Mitgliedern des Balletcorps.

Herr Kapellmeister Gyrowetz hat die Leitung dieser Akademie, und Herr Philipp von Stubenrauch die Anordnung der Tableaux übernommen.
Die Einnahme wird von der Gesellschaft adeliger Frauen zur Beförderung ihrer wohlthätigen Zwecke verwendet.

Sämmtlichen Personen, welche mit der menschenfreundlichsten Bereitwilligkeit ihre Talente und Bemühungen gewidmet haben, wird hiermit der verbindlichste Dank abgestattet.
Die Eintrittspreise sind wie gewöhnlich. Die Freybilletten sind ohne Ausnahme ungültig.
Die gesperrten Sitze sind an der k. k. Hoftheater = Casse, die Logen aber bey der Frau Therese Landgräfinn von Fürstenberg, geb. Fürstinn von Schwarzenberg, in der Himmelpfortgasse im Fürstenbergischen Hause Nro. 952. im 2. Stock zu haben.

Der Anfang ist um 7 Uhr.

The programme of a charity concert organised by Josef Sonnleithner in 1821, in which three of Schubert's works had their first public performance: *Erlkönig*, the quartet *Das Dörfchen*, and the song *Der Gesang der Geister über den Wassern*.

their favours to Haydn and Mozart helped and admired Beethoven, though he was a difficult protégé. He was no longer a 'favoured servant' as Haydn had been in Eisenstadt. Beethoven was a respected guest in the palaces of the Liechtensteins, Schwarzenbergs, Waldstein, Lichnowskys, Galitzins. They were often awed by him.

When Schubert grew up the aristocrats around Beethoven took no notice of the young 'compositeur' of songs. He did not mind. He was happy with his friends and inspired by them. Times were not good in Vienna; the short boom after the Congress had come to an end and everybody was complaining. *Raunzen* was always a favourite Viennese pastime. In 1819 the police recorded an 'exceptionally high' number of suicides in Vienna. And in 1819 Schubert wrote the *Trout* Quintet, one of his best loved works, full of joy and happiness.

It had been commissioned by his musical patron in Steyr, Sylvester Paumgartner, a good amateur player (cello and wind instruments). He loved Schubert's *Lied, Die Forelle*, often had it sung at his musical soirées and once asked Schubert, who happened to be there, to turn it into some chamber music. Schubert nodded, sat down and wrote this masterpiece for piano and four strings (violin, viola, cello, double bass). He knew Johann Nepomuk Hummel's *Grande Quintuor* for the same combination and he was attracted by contrasting the piano against the strings. The song is used as a middle movement with variations. The song movement is not isolated, however, but forms the structure of the entire work built around it. The *Trout* Quintet is a musical poem born out of the Austrian landscape; the lovely song *Die Forelle* remains its focus. Schubert was always thinking of song melodies. The *Trout* Quintet was published as Op. 114 by Joseph Czerny a year after Schubert's death. Its charm remains constant and contagious. It has a slight drawback though for amateur chamber players; often it is difficult to find a congenial double bass player.

'I have done little new in the way of songs but I have tried my hand at several instrumental works. I have written two quartets ... and an octet, and I intend to write another quartet. In this manner I want to pave my way to another grand symphony ...' Schubert wrote to Leopold Kupelwieser on 31 March 1824.

All chamber music players love Schubert's A minor and D minor Quartets. The A minor was the only of his famous quartets which Schubert saw published in his lifetime. He wrote it in February and March 1824. It was performed on 14 March by the Schuppanzigh Quartet – Schuppanzigh, Holz, Weiss, Linke. According to Schwind they played it 'rather slowly, with great purity and tenderness', but Schubert was unhappy with the performance. It was published under Op. 29, No. 1 on 7 December. It is now considered the true expression of Schubert's wide ranging genius, with its melancholy, exuberant and always melodious moments. The Leipzig *Allgemeine musikalische Zeitung* admitted condescendingly, 'As a first attempt it is not to be despised.' That author was not aware that it was closer to Schubert's thirteenth chamber music attempt. What should have been Op. 29, No. 2 – the D minor Quartet – was published posthumously. The great G major Quartet that was to be Op. 29, No. 3 is now known as Op. 161. It was published in 1850, twenty-two years after Schubert's death.

opposite Karl Freiherr
von Schoenstein.

The A minor Quartet, a genuine jewel, belongs to the gold reserve of all string quartet players. The slow movement was taken from the Andantino in *Rosamunde*, a common practice in Schubert's days. Both the Andantino and the following Minuet are true *Lieder* without words, written for string quartet, wistful and singing. For his D minor Quartet Schubert expanded his *Lied, Der Tod und das Mädchen*, into a theme with variations. (In his Quartet K. 575, one of the 'solo' quartets dedicated to the cello-playing King of Prussia, Friedrich Wilhelm II, Mozart used his song *Das Veilchen* (The Violet) for the slow movement.) The D minor Quartet is one of Schubert's most important works. At the age of twenty-seven, when he wrote it, the thought of death was already much in his mind.

Much has been said about Schubert's attitude to death. He often thinks of death in his *Lieder* and instrumental music. Unlike the mystic German *Todessehnsucht* (the death wish), the theme of Wagner's *Tristan und Isolde*, Schubert has a friendlier, more intimate relationship to death: death is inevitable, one has to live with the thought. It is basically a Viennese attitude, more practical than profound, very widespread today. Sell my clothes, I'm going to heaven. It is a sort of Occidental fatalism, and it has served the Viennese well in the course of their many disasters. One hears it in Schubert's melancholy moments, in *An die Nachtigall*, in the *Winterreise* cycle, in the second movement of the *Unfinished* Symphony, in the D minor Quartet.

Schubert showed admirable courage when he wrote his A minor and D minor quartets, after Beethoven had completed his 'middle' quartets Op. 59, Op. 74 and Op. 95. Schubert seems almost unconcerned about Beethoven who was then thinking of his late, great quartets. As a good composer Schubert must have understood the almost perfect structure of Beethoven's Quartet Op. 59, No. 1, the amazing first movement and the Adagio that is 'typical' Beethoven. What he thought of it we do not know. But he did write his chamber musical masterpieces only as he could write them. No one claims that the A minor is technically a perfect quartet. But it is Schubert through and through.

The third of his great quartets, in G major, was written in ten days, from 20 June to 30 June 1826. Amazing because it is almost an 'orchestral' work, with unison passages, agitated tremoli, and a powerful structure that seems to precede Bruckner. 'Except that Bruckner never wrote a movement of such lively construction and such unity of design,' Albert Einstein writes about the opening movement of Schubert's G major. The 'slightly agitated' Andante is another song without words which may have influenced Brahms in his elegiac moods. The Scherzo with its wistful *Ländler* melody is great Viennese music.

Schubert thought highly of this work and he selected the first movement of the G major Quartet to be performed at the only Private Concert of his life, on 26 March 1828, eight months before his death. Schuppanzigh was ill and the first violin part was played by the excellent violinist J. M. Böhm with Holz, Weiss and Linke. The reaction of the audience was favourable; no wonder since the audience consisted mostly of enthusiastic Schubertians. The critic of the Leipzig *Allgemeine musikalische Zeitung* praised the movement's 'spirit and originality'.

Schubert, not sophisticated in his relations with women, deeply and truly understood the mysteries of a woman's heart. How else could he have written *Gretchen am Spinnrade?* Women have always been moved by Schubert's 'Meine Ruh' ist hin', as they are moved by Shakespeare's Juliet and Goethe's Gretchen. That Schubert could express a woman's feelings so well in music is in contrast with his shy and clumsy behaviour when he met a woman in life. His biographers are often puzzled about his relationship with women. Schubert himself, very reticent in his private affairs, is not much help. Some writers have romantically 'expanded' the few facts that are known which only confuses the matter. He was in love – more than once – that much we know. But his love mostly remained unfulfilled; that too is part of the record. But why? What was wrong? Could it be that the girls he was in love with sensed that his only real passion was his music? 'Not a single love letter from Schubert survives and perhaps none ever existed,' says O. E. Deutsch. Schubert was too shy to write about his intimate feelings.

In 1814, when Schubert was seventeen, Therese Grob, a girl from his neighbourhood, sang the soprano solo in his earliest Mass in F major which he had written that year, between 17 May and 22 July. (We always seem to know more about the exact dates than the emotional origin of his works; he meticulously put down the dates but rarely spoke about his feelings.) The F major Mass was performed on 16 October, at the centenary of the parish church in Liechtental where he had been baptized and later sang as a choirboy and learned the rudiments of church music. Schubert conducted the Mass from the organ. He did so again ten days later at the Augustiner Church.

Therese Grob's mother ran a small silk shop near the parish church. Her father had come to Vienna from Switzerland. She was one year younger than Schubert and he fell in love with her. She was no beauty. Schubert's classmate, Anton Holzapfel, described her as rather plump, with a round child's face and pock marks. Anselm Hüttenbrenner, often unreliable as a source, remembered that Schubert told him, after it was all over:

Therese Grob.

131

I loved her very deeply and she loved me ... She wasn't pretty but she was good; she had kindness of heart. For three years I hoped to marry her but I could find no position that would keep us both provided for. She married someone else and I was deeply hurt. I am still in love with her, and since then no other woman has pleased me as much. But she wasn't for me.

The touch of sentimental resignation, typical of Schubert, is there, but the story sounds rather as though Hüttenbrenner in his old age, when he began to remember, had indulged in another fantasy. Somehow the reminiscence fails to ring true. Schubert would not have talked about a 'position that would keep us both provided for'. Holzapfel, another of doubtful memory, writes that Schubert had admitted to him his love 'in a long, enthusiastic, unfortunately lost letter'. That might have happened. Schubert was always reluctant to talk about intimate matters. Holzapfel replied in a long letter to Schubert, trying to talk him out of what he (Holzapfel) calls 'his ridiculous infatuation'. In 1815 and 1816, when he was in love with Therese, Schubert wrote many beautiful love songs – that is a fact – and it is quite possible that some were written for her. She often sang his new songs from manuscript and Schubert accompanied her on the piano. It was a tender love story; he was seventeen, she was one year younger. During the night following the first performance of the F major Mass, in which Therese had sung the soprano solo, Schubert composed Schiller's *Das Mädchen aus der Fremde*: 'Beseligend war ihre Nähe/und alle Herzen wurden weit ...' (Blissful was her nearness/and all hearts opened ...) It could have been the shy declaration of a boy in love.

On 21 November 1820 Therese Grob and the master baker Johann Bergmann were married at the Liechtental parish church. If she had loved Schubert she had decided against him in favour of security. A master baker could offer her a safer life than a struggling composer. Thirty-eight years later Anselm Hüttenbrenner talked to Ferdinand Luib who was collecting material for a Schubert biography. Hüttenbrenner said, 'From the time he lost the girl he had loved, Schubert showed much antipathy toward other girls.' This statement was never confirmed by the facts. Hüttenbrenner also told Luib, 'Schubert was a rather a cold fish (*ein trockener Patron*) towards the other sex and not exactly gallant man. He paid no attention to his clothes, or to his teeth, he smelled of tobacco and was not qualified for a suitor, not *salonfähig*'. The memories of a bitter old eccentric.

Schubert's fondness for tobacco has been confirmed by others; when he felt 'inspired' he liked a smoke and a glass of wine. His friends often saw him late in the morning, still in bed, surrounded by music paper and manuscripts. He liked working early in the morning, and like a certain British

statesman, he liked working in bed. Sometimes Schubert kept his glasses on at night to be ready for working in the morning as soon as he woke up.

Schubert was relaxed about his manuscripts. Unfortunately, Anselm Hüttenbrenner remembered:

When friends arrived for whom Schubert sang his new *Lieder* they often took the manuscripts and promised to return them soon which did not always happen though. Often Schubert did not know where his manuscripts were. Then my brother Josef, who lived with him, began to collect the lost songs. He succeeded after many researches. I saw one day that my brother kept over a hundred Schubert *Lieder* in a drawer. Schubert was pleased and gave my brother all new *Lieder* while they lived together under one roof.

Even more doubtful are Schubert's alleged feelings for Caroline, the young Countess Esterházy. He wrote some songs for her, such as *Ungeduld* in *Die schöne Müllerin*. The rest is conjecture. He certainly realized that he and Caroline lived on different planets, socially speaking. He was always a realist. Towards the end of his life he and Caroline became almost friends. She was always interested in his work; Bauernfeld, the poet, alluded to this elegantly: 'The conflict between a full life and spiritual creation is always difficult, unless there is a balance in the soul. In the case of our friend, an ideal love had a conciliatory, balancing influence.'

Sooner or later Schubert seems to have resigned himself to being a bachelor. He was not the only bachelor-composer who was always married to his music: Beethoven, Brahms, Bruckner are others. Perhaps he did try to find a substitute 'love' in his affair, if there ever was one, with 'the pretty housemaid' in Zseliz. One fact remains: Schubert who wrote some of the most beautiful love songs of musical literature, whose *Lieder* have inspired and comforted generations of happy and unhappy lovers, knew little love in his own life.

Schubert was and remained a nonconformist. He was deeply religious – only such a man could have written the great Masses in A flat major and E flat major, the finest works of this kind since Beethoven, that were later followed by Bruckner's D minor and F minor Masses – but he had no use for the hierarchy of the Roman Catholic Church. 'Schubert,' wrote Anselm Hüttenbrenner, 'had a devout nature and believed firmly in God and the immortality of the soul; his religion is clearly expressed in many of his songs.'

Schubert's problem was to conceal his deep-set dislike of Austrian clericalism. He had frequent quarrels with his father, an orthodox believer. He sided with his oldest brother, Ignaz, a freethinker who referred to priests as the *Bonzen*, the big shots. During his first summer in Hungary Schubert had

opposite The interior of the Old Burgtheater in Vienna; watercolour by Gustav Klimt.

angry letters from Ignaz who complained about the 'fat-headed *Bonzen*', and that 'the pupils no longer dare laugh when I tell them a funny story about superstitions in the Scripture class'. In a postscript to his letter Ignaz warned his brother not to mention any religious matter in his replies to him or to their father. Schubert ignored the warning. 'You, Ignaz,' he wrote admiringly, 'are still quite the old man of iron. Your implacable hatred of the whole tribe of *Bonzen* does you credit. You have no idea what a gang the priesthood is here . . .'

In the 1820s Catholic societies and religious orders, with the active support of Metternich's reactionary government, made an effort to win back some of the influence they had lost during the enlightened régime of Emperor Joseph II. A generation before the Church had worried about the influence of the Freemasons. (Mozart had joined this body of men.) But when Schubert grew up there were more effective outlets against clericalism: romantic poetry; love of Nature; Goethe's pantheistic influence. Schubert even saw a Christmas tree in the house of his friend, Moritz von Schwind. Though Schwind had been educated by Benedictine teachers at the Schotten School in Vienna he was, and remained, a fierce anti-cleric. He quarrelled with the orthodox beliefs of his fiancée and at one point told her to go and fall in love with the Pope. He wrote this in a letter to Bauernfeld, who liked the remark so well that he used it later in a comedy. Eventually the engagement was called off.

Schubert's real feelings are apparent in his beautiful church music. 'Schubert did omit the words *Et unam Sanctam catholicam et apostolicam ecclesiam* from his Masses but of course not the *Credo* proper,' O. E. Deutsch comments. In their strictest meaning Schubert's masses were not intended for liturgical use. But they are sung in many churches because of their sheer beauty.

In 1825 he wrote to his father that his new songs from Walter Scott's *Lady of the Lake* had much success in Gmunden.

They wondered greatly at my piety which I expressed in a hymn to the Holy Virgin and which, it appears, grips every soul and turns it to devotion. I think it is due to the fact that I have never forced devotion in myself and never compose hymns or prayers of that kind unless it overcomes me unawares. But then it is usually the right and true devotion.

The Hymn to the Holy Virgin, well known as *Ave Maria*, became very popular and was often transcribed; and four months before his death Schubert composed the Hebrew text of the 92nd Psalm for Chief Cantor Salomon Sulzer of the Vienna Synagogue. Sulzer had approached Schubert for his contribution, a solo for the Cantor's baritone voice and the chorus. This too showed 'the right and true devotion'.

opposite A page from Schubert's diary, 1816: 'This will remain a bright, beautiful day throughout my life.' (See p. 140)

~~16.~~ 13. Juny 1816.

Ein heller, lichter, schöner Tag wird
dieser durch mein ganzes Leben bleiben. Wie von ferne leise hallen
mir noch die Zaubertöne von Mozarts
Musik. ~~Und~~ Wie unglaublich kräftig
u. wieder so sanft ward's durch Schle-
singers meisterhaftes Spiel ins
Herz tief, tief eingedrückt. So
bleiben uns diese schöne Abdrücke
in der Seele, welche ~~Zeit~~ keine
Zeit, keine Umstände verwischen,
u. wohlthätig auf unser Daseyn
wirken. Sie zeigen uns in der Fin-
sterniss dieses Lebens eine lichte,
helle, schöne Ferne, worauf wir mit
Zuversicht ~~hoffen~~. O Mozart,

Schubert kept diaries but most of them are lost. An exception is the diary of 1816 which is kept in the archives of the Gesellschaft der Musikfreunde and in the Stadtbibliothek. It was first published in Kreissle's biography in 1865. The first entry is written on 13 June 1816:

This will remain a bright, beautiful day throughout my life. The magic tones of Mozart's music are still reverberating in my ears. Schlesinger's masterful playing made a strong and tender impression in my heart. Neither the progress of time nor the circumstances will wipe out these impressions in my soul; they show us in the darkness of this life a bright and beautiful distance that gives us hope. Dear Mozart, immortal Mozart, how many such miraculous impressions of a lighter, better life did you make in our souls ... This quintet is one of his greatest 'small' works ... I too had to perform at this occasion. I played Variations by Beethoven, I sang Goethe's *Rastlose Liebe* and Schiller's *Amalia*. The first song had more applause than the second. One cannot deny that much of the applause was due to Goethe's musical poet-genius ...

That was Schubert's first impression after Mozart's magnificent G minor String Quintet K. 516, which Hans Keller describes as being 'as great as the G Minor Symphony, whence it is greater ... the same wealth of feeling expressed more economically in the chamber work'. Schubert, then nineteen, had clearly captured the greatness of Mozart's genius. The following day, 14 June, Schubert wrote in his diary:

After several months I made once again an evening promenade. There is hardly anything more pleasant than to walk on a warm evening in the meadows between Währing and Döbling. In doubtful twilight, in the company of my brother Carl, I felt well. The cemetery was nearby and we were thinking of our dear mother....

On 8 September the young man confided to his diary some private thoughts:

A man is like a ball. Accidents and passions play with him. The sentence seems to me very truthful. Writers often say, 'The world is a stage, and everybody plays his part'.

Applause or censure follow in another world. But a part is given, and each of us plays a part, and who can tell whether he plays it well or badly?

Nature and education define a person's mind and heart. The heart is the ruler but it should be the mind. Take people as they are, not as they should be.

Happy is the man who finds a true friend. Happier he who finds a wife who is also a true friend.

A man suffers unhappiness without complaining but he feels it deeply inside ...

Now I know nothing anymore. Tomorrow I may again know something. Why? Could it be that my mind is less sharp than tomorrow because I am sleepy? Why doesn't my mind go on working when the body sleeps? Does the mind take a walk? Because it cannot sleep. Strange questions, they will say ... Good night, until we wake again.

Eight years later on 25 March 1824 Schubert confided similar thoughts to another diary which is lost:

Suffering sharpens the mind and strengthens the heart. Happiness however rarely touches the mind and makes the heart frivolous.

And two days later on 27 March:

No one understands somebody else's unhappiness or joy. People think they go toward each other but they only walk next to each other. How sad for the man who realizes it!... My work is created through my understanding of music and my suffering: those works that were created mostly by suffering don't seem to please the world.

O. E. Deutsch comments that Schubert's thoughts reminded him of Shelley's 'Men learn in suffering what they teach in songs' and 'Our sweetest songs are those that tell of saddest thought'.

A strange entry is undated, saying 'two o'clock in the morning: Enviable Nero! How strong you were, to ruin people with string music and song!'

Opera: Unhappy Love Affair

The infatuation of the Viennese with the stage goes back for centuries. In the 1620s the Jesuits staged Miracle and Passion plays, in Latin, but they were certain to include German language *intermezzi* by way of 'educating' their audiences. They knew that the direct path to the hearts and minds of the people led through the theatre. Later the great moralists would use the stage to spread their message among the listeners. In Vienna baroque opera became entertainment, education and a symbol of absolutism. 'Spectacles are necessary,' said Josef von Sonnenfels, Maria Theresia's Minister of Justice, and the Empress agreed.

Nearly all composers living in Vienna hoped to write for the stage and Schubert, the genuine Viennese child, was no exception. He was deeply interested in the theatre, especially the opera. Italian opera still dominated Vienna, particularly the upper classes, but there were the beginnings of German opera and the Singspiel. In 1782 Mozart wrote *Die Entführung aus dem Serail* and in 1791 *Die Zauberflöte*. In 1814 Schubert was at the Theater an der Wien when Beethoven had a great success at last with his revision of *Fidelio*. And in 1821 there was a triumph for Weber's *Der Freischütz*.

Schubert wrote what he naïvely thought was his first 'opera', *Des Teufels Lustschloss* (The Devil's Country Palace), before he was seventeen and he discussed an operatic libretto with his friends Bauernfeld and Lachner two days before his death. All his life he suffered from the failures of his 'wretched operas'. He left a dozen operas and operatic fragments. They contain musical gems but are dramatically unsound. Schubert was a born melodist and lyricist but he never understood the strict laws of the musical stage.

In 1815, after the failure of *Des Teufels Lustschloss*, Schubert wrote four operatic works. He worked almost as fast as Donizetti or Rossini but less successfully. Between 8 and 19 May he wrote *Der vierjährige Posten*, after a libretto by the patriotic Austrian poet Theodor Körner, author of the popular war poems *Leyer und Schwert*. Between 27 June and 9 July he wrote the one-act ballad opera *Fernando*. It had been written by Albert Stadler, his friend from the old days at the Stadtkonvikt.

opposite The Kärnthertor Theater, where 'Die Zwillingsbrüder' was first performed in June 1820.

145

Next Schubert tried a Singspiel after a libretto by Goethe, *Claudine von Villa Bella*. Some of his friends really liked it but unfortunately only the first act survives. The score of the second and third acts was used by the servants of Josef Hüttenbrenner to light a fire one day in 1848. Finally, towards the end of the year, Schubert wrote the music to *Die Freunde von Salamanca*. The author, his friend Mayrhofer, was a dilettante poet but no dramatist. The plot of the libretto is an involved intrigue between a Countess Olivia and her various suitors. There are such silly lines as

The playbill for 'Die Zwillingsbrüder'.

> The shepherd by the silver stream
> Beneath the greenwood's leafy tent.
> Of his fair love doth sit and dream
> And yearning sings his sad lament.

Alas, Schubert, who understood poetry, knew nothing about a good libretto. Among the melodies he created is one that he used later in his Octet as a theme with variations – thus *Salamanca* was not a total loss. All this happened in 1815 when Schubert also wrote over 150 *Lieder*, among them the marvellous *Erlkönig* and *Heidenröslein*.

Only one of his stage works, the one-act Singspiel *Die Zwillingsbrüder* (The Twin Brothers), was produced in his lifetime. The libretto had been 'adapted from the French' by Georg Ernst Hofmann, secretary of the Theater an der Wien. It was performed in June 1820 at the Kärntnertor Theater, probably owing to the considerable influence of Johann Michael Vogl, Schubert's friend, who sang the leading part. It was hardly more than a *succès d'estime*. All of Schubert's friends, and their friends, went to hear the 'farcical comedy with music' and worked as an enthusiastic clique. The critic of the Leipzig *Allgemeine musikalische Zeitung* wrote:

That Herr Schubert has many friends who were also very active in promoting him was evident at the first performance. But they may have forgotten that between *fiasco* and *furore*, as the Italians say, there is a tremendous difference. For the beginner, friendly encouragement is the finest, most beneficial reward, and here as everywhere the middle way is always the best.

The work disappeared after a few performances. It was the same story all over again: Schubert wrote beautiful melodies but had no sense of drama. While he was thinking of the stage the Viennese had heard the operas of Gluck, Cherubini's *Faniska*, Mozart's *Don Giovanni*, and the greatest local successes *Waisenhaus* and *Schweizerfamilie*, two long forgotten works by Joseph Weigl. Schubert might have heard Cherubini's *Medea*, Spontini's *Vestale* and Boïeldieu's *Jean de Paris*, but he never bothered to really study the Italian *opera seria* and *opera buffa*. He was young and he wanted to sing. With the exception of Mozart, the greatest musical genius of all, the composers of the musical-dramatic masterpieces were older men who had learned their lessons the hard way and had the experience of a lifetime: Monteverdi, Gluck, Verdi, Wagner.

Schubert had read some of Shakespeare's works but, unlike Verdi, he failed to understand the genius of the powerful dramatist. Bauernfeld had made a German translation of *Two Gentlemen of Verona* and, with Mayrhofer, of *Cleopatra* for a Viennese printer and publisher named Josef Trensentzky who put out an edition of Shakespeare. Schwind contributed some vignettes. Schubert saw the edition in 1826 and turned three Shakespeare poems into songs. The most famous of them, the Serenade from *Cymbeline* (*Ständchen*), was based on August Wilhelm Schlegel's translation. It has become one of Schubert's best known *Lieder*. Why did he not feel inspired more often by

Eduard von Bauernfeld.

below The playwright and actor Ferdinand Raimund, and (*left*) as he appeared on stage.

Shakespeare? *Fool's Songs* and *Songs of Ophelia* were available in Vienna in German translations. Fischer-Dieskau believes that Schubert may have felt 'a strange shyness' towards the great dramatist.

Schubert's addiction to melody need not have prevented his success on the stage if he had learned to use the melodies to explain characters and advance the drama. Verdi, the great melodist of opera, gave the people melodies as well as drama. The melodies were remembered but the drama held everything together. When the Duke of Mantua sings 'La donna è mobile' in the last act of *Rigoletto* one both understands his character and wants to know what is going to happen.

Schubert wanted to write 'German opera'. But neither *Die Zauberflöte* nor *Der Freischütz*, produced in Vienna in November 1821, expressed Schubert's ideas of 'German opera', which were closer to the Singspiel, the classical operetta. As a *Lied* composer his instinct was unfailing. Goethe was his greatest poet and through the wealth of his musical imagination Schubert ennobled all poems he set to music, even many that were far below Goethe's art. But the opera librettist whom Schubert admired was August von Kotzebue – a long way from Goethe even though Kotzebue happened to be born in Weimar. Kotzebue was the most popular playwright in Vienna when Schubert was born. He knew what the people wanted and gave them comedies and tragedies. He was frivolous, sentimental and often trite. He had written *Des Teufels Lustschloss*, Schubert's first operatic venture. He was also the author of *Der Spiegelritter*, another operatic fragment by Schubert. He had definite ideas about writing a libretto. When *Der Spiegelritter* had been set to music in 1791 by one Ignaz Walter, in Frankfurt am Main, Kotzebue had written:

People have often asked me to write an opera in the modern manner, and now at last I have done so. I trust that the readers will find it just as droll, romantic and silly as its older brothers and sisters on the German stage. Of all an author's works this sort of opera is the easiest to write.

And the easiest to forget.

No one has explained why Schubert never turned towards the poet and playwright in Vienna who might have understood him, Ferdinand Raimund. They had much in common. Both have been called 'typical' Biedermeier characters though they were anything but Biedermeier. Raimund, born seven years before Schubert, was the son of a cabinet maker who had come from Prague to Vienna and married a Viennese girl. Young Ferdinand began as an apprentice confectioner, selling pastries in the gallery of the Burgtheater, and there he fell hopelessly in love with the stage. He became a celebrated actor and wrote plays in which he starred. A gentle poet, subtle and serious, he was often misunderstood. He too had a hard life when he grew up and he wrote about the things he knew best, Vienna and the Viennese. After 1823 he was famous as a local playwright but even more as an actor. Actors always were, and still are, more popular than playwrights in Vienna. Raimund might have been Schubert's ideal librettist since they shared so many things together, but they never co-operated. They seem to have met only once, at Beethoven's funeral, when Schubert was too upset to think of future projects.

Not unlike Schubert Raimund, in his greatness, was only discovered many years after his death; he committed suicide in 1836. At last it was realized that the popular comedian had been a sensitive poet. Grillparzer, whose plays were performed on the stage of the Burgtheater, admitted there was 'some genius' in Raimund's plays. But Ferdinand Raimund was performed at the Burgtheater only after his death. Hofmannsthal wrote that 'something dark and sinister always stands next to Raimund'. Sentiment, despair and resignation are softened by moments of Viennese cheerfulness. One cannot help thinking that Raimund and Schubert might have worked well together. Hans Gal believes an 'immortal work' might have resulted from a play by Raimund with music by Schubert and concludes, 'This too belongs to the unfulfilled possibilities which accompanied Schubert's life.' Or Raimund's.

Similarly, it is odd that Schubert did not know Nestroy – Johann Nepomuk Eduard Ambrosius Nestroy, who sounds exactly like a character out of one of his own plays. Nestroy was born in Vienna in 1801, four years after Schubert; he studied jurisprudence but gave it up when the court opera engaged him as a bass-baritone. He had great success as Sarastro in *The Magic Flute* and sang Schubert's music as a member of a male chorus. Unfortunately they never met. Nestroy later lost his singing voice, became a comedian and began to write popular Viennese comedies in which he starred. In no time Vienna's critics and audiences were divided into partisans of Raimund and fans of Nestroy and the legend of their enmity was widespread, though modern research has not proved it.

Nestroy became famous in 1833 with his fairy-tale farce *Lumpazivaga-bundus*. Schubert had then been dead for five years and was remembered only by his family and his numerous friends. Not unlike Schubert, Nestroy revolted against the smug Biedermeier attitude of many Viennese. In his comedy *Zu ebener Erde und erster Stock* (Ground Floor and First Floor) Nestroy ridiculed the *Backhendlzeit*, the Fried Chicken Era, when chicken fried in bread crumbs became the dish for special occasions. Nestroy, somewhat like Schubert's friend Bauernfeld, had no use for the snobbery of the nouveau rich. But the *Backhendlzeit* came later, after the *Schubertiaden*. Schubert's

above The bass-baritone singer Johann Nestroy and (*left*) on stage.

friends, such as Spaun and Schober, were relaxed about titles and proper addresses. They were not insecure, like the characters of Nestroy; they preferred the company of their friend Schubert. Nestroy had a strong sense of the stage and there is no saying what might have happened if he had met Schubert and written a play for him.

In 1821 Domenico Barbaja, a flamboyant impresario from the San Carlo Theatre in Naples, was given a twelve-year contract by the Vienna authorities to manage the Court Opera at the Kärntnertor Theater. Barbaja brought some excellent Italian companies to Vienna. His star attraction was the much admired Rossini who arrived in 1822 accompanied by his wife, the famous soprano Isabella Colbran. Rossini became the toast of the town. While he was in Vienna the local composers, including Beethoven, were ignored. Barbaja gave the Viennese what they wanted, good Italian opera. 'A large section of German opinion, among them Franz Schubert, was perfectly ready to concede the superiority of Italian opera, even though Italian competition had taken a disastrous roll of Schubert's own efforts in that particular field,' writes Heinrich Kralik in *The Vienna Opera*.

Barbaja approached Carl Maria von Weber. *Der Freischütz* was the only work able to compete with the magic of Rossini. Weber was invited to come to Vienna to write *Euryanthe* for the Vienna Opera. It was produced there in October 1823 but did not have the great success of *Der Freischütz*. Weber met Schubert and liked him. Schubert's latest opera was *Alfonso and Estrella*, after a libretto by Schubert's friend Schober. They had worked on it together in St Pölten in the autumn of 1821, in the house of Bishop Johann Nepomuk von Dankesreither. Schubert wrote to Spaun that he and Schober 'had great hopes of it'. But *Alfonso and Estrella*, a romantic love story, was not very good.

Spaun remembers:

Weber promised to get *Alfonso and Estrella* produced in Berlin under his direction. Schubert was at Weber's almost every day. They had become very close friends. But after the first performance of *Euryanthe* Weber asked Schubert how he had liked it. Schubert, always sincere and truthful, said that while he liked some of it, it contained too little melody for him, and that he liked the *Freischütz* very much better. Weber was offended, answered ungraciously, and there was no further mention of Schubert's opera.

This may be partly correct. Schubert wrote to Spaun on 7 December 1822, 'I had no luck with the opera in Vienna. Vogl has left the theatre too. In the near future I shall send it to Dresden whence I have received a very promising letter from Weber, or to Berlin ... I should be quite well if this wretched business of the opera were not so mortifying.' But the name of Schubert never appears in Weber's letters. Apparently he had dismissed Schubert completely.

Then Anna Milder-Hauptmann, the famous singer and Beethoven's first Fidelio, asked Schubert to send her an opera since 'she gathered he had written several'. Schubert submitted to her *Alfonso and Estrella*. On 8 March 1825 Milder-Hauptmann wrote to him saying she was extremely sorry 'that the libretto does not correspond with the local taste. People here (in Berlin) are accustomed to grand tragic opera or French comic opera.' And she added, 'If I am to have the pleasure of being able to appear in one of your operas it would certainly have to be suited to my personality....' Once a singer, always a singer. Schubert asked her to return the opera. He tried once more in 1827 when he sent the score to Graz. Nothing came of it. The work was performed only in 1882 in Vienna, fifty-four years after Schubert's death.

Schubert had no better luck with 'the heroic, romantic opera' *Fierabras*

above Rossini, who visited Vienna in 1822.

below Carl Maria von Weber.

which he wrote in the spring and summer of 1823 (the year in which he also wrote the beautiful song cycle *Die schöne Müllerin*). The libretto was written by Schubert's friend Josef Kupelwieser, secretary at the Kärntnertor Theater. Schubert never learned that good friends are not necessarily good librettists. The plot is utter nonsense, borrowed from an old French romance *Fierabras* (The Braggart). The cast of characters includes an evil Moorish prince called Boland. The music was not much better than the plot. Again we are confronted by the mystery of Schubert's producing such a score at the time when he may have been thinking of the melodious beauty of *Die schöne Müllerin*.

The opera singer Anna Milder-Hauptmann.

Also in 1823 Schubert wrote the score of *Die Verschworenen* (The Conspirators). It was later re-titled *Der häusliche Krieg* (The Domestic War). The censors would not permit anything having to do with conspirators. This time a professional playwright, Ignaz Franz Castelli, wrote the libretto, after Aristophanes' comedy *Lysistrata*. Aristophanes' masterpiece was performed in Athens in 411 BC, a brilliant political satire about the strong-minded women who refuse to sleep with their husbands until the men will stop the foolishness of going to war. Castelli changed the Acropolis in Athens into a mediaeval castle at the time of the Crusades – there had to be a mention of the Crusades – and made the formidable Lysistrata the wife of a German baron! There is a conspiracy among the chorus of women led by the wife of the baron. Some have described this effort as 'a parody of grand opera', but Schubert was quite serious when he wrote the music. It is a conventional score with some good moments. It was never performed while Schubert was alive, but many times later on. Apparently Castelli knew what he was doing.

Schubert became upset about his operatic failures. On 31 March 1824 he wrote to Leopold Kupelwieser:

The opera *Fierabras* by your brother [who acted unwisely by leaving his job at the Kärntnertor Theater] was declared unusable, and consequently the music was not required either. Castelli's libretto *Die Verschworenen* has been set to music by a Berlin composer and was received with applause there. So it would again seem that I have written two operas in vain.

Schubert fails to mention the name of the Berlin composer and he was not surprised that Castelli gave the same libretto to various composers.

So much for Schubert's operas. He also wrote incidental music to two plays. There was no singing, just a few musical interludes here and there. *Die Zauberharfe* (The Magic Harp) was written in 1820 by Georg Ernst Hofmann, the librettist of Schubert's earlier *Die Zwillingsbrüder*. Little is known about it. The other play was *Rosamunde, Fürstin von Zypern*, a romantic drama by Helmine von Chezy who is remembered for having written the libretto

153

of *Euryanthe*. Bauernfeld described her as 'extremely good-natured, a little ridiculous, and not particularly distinguished for her cleanliness'.

Having done the libretto of Weber's *Euryanthe* Frau von Chézy came to Vienna and wrote 'a new drama with choruses' to which, according to the magazine *Der Sammler* (The Collector) of 18 December 1823, 'the well-known and talented composer, Herr Franz Schubert' had written the incidental music. It was gossiped that Josef Kupelwieser was in love with Mlle Emilie Neumann, the star of the Theater an der Wien, and had persuaded his friend Schubert to write the music. Schubert wrote to Frau von Chézy that he had been convinced of the merit of *Rosamunde* 'the moment he read it'.

The critics wrote that the romantic drama was silly and quite improbable. But some of the nine pieces of the incidental music are so good that they have survived the efforts of latter-day arrangers. For the première at the Theater an der Wien on 20 December 1823 Schubert used his overture to *Alfonso and Estrella*. Later he replaced it by the overture to *Die Zauberharfe* which was published in a version for two pianos as *Overture to Rosamunde*, which it remains to this day. Exchanging one's overtures had been the practice with the prolific Italians, Rossini and Donizetti. Mozart knew better; he would not have used the *Figaro* Overture for *Così fan tutte*, or vice versa.

Schubert was ill and does not seem to have attended the première. Schwind was there but his account is not very helpful. He notes that 'a ballet passed unnoticed'. The ballet music is now extremely popular. Schwind also wrote that the second and third entractes also 'passed unnoticed'. He liked the Andantino in the fourth act which he called 'a short Bucolic'. It was followed by applause. Schubert knew it was good; he later used the Andantino for the slow movement of the wonderful A minor Quartet and again in the Variations of one of his Impromptus. One section, played by the wood-winds, later appears in his *Ständchen*. In the fourth act Schwind noticed 'a chorus by shepherds and huntsmen, so beautiful and natural, that I do not remember ever having heard anything like it'. This chorus too was repeated. Schwind, the faithful friend, hoped 'it would deal the chorus from Weber's *Euryanthe* the sort of blow it deserves'. Schubert's friends were fiercely loyal to him. The Divertissement *alla tirolese*, with its many fine harmonic ideas, became one of the most popular parts of the score – but only much, much later. *Rosamunde* was performed only twice. The critic of *Der Sammler* wrote that Herr Schubert had shown originality in his score, unfortunately also eccentricity.

For many years the music to *Rosamunde* was forgotten. In 1867 two Schubert enthusiasts from England, Sir George Grove and Sir Arthur Sullivan, discovered the music in Vienna 'in a pile of manuscripts' owned by Schubert's nephew, Eduard Schneider. However the incidental music to *Rosamunde* had been mentioned two years earlier in the Schubert biography published by Heinrich Kreissle von Hellborn. The Schubert enthusiasts from England were correct though. The Overture and the Incidental Music have survived in many transcriptions. The *Rosamunde* music remains glorious proof of the popular side of Schubert's genius.

'Here, Here Is My End'

On 14 August 1823 Schubert wrote to Schober from Steyr, 'I feel fairly well again. But I almost doubt whether I shall ever be completely healthy.' He knew he was incurably ill, and he had moments of despair, a deep longing for death. He avoided being with people; he avoided even his friends. Beethoven's nephew Karl wrote in his *Conversations-Hefte*, 'Everyone speaks very highly of Schubert but he seems to have gone into hiding.'

The friends were worried. On 8 November Schwind wrote that all the friends attended a farewell party for Leopold Kupelwieser, the painter who was going to Rome 'except Schubert who was confined to bed that day ... Schaeffer and Bernard who visited him assured us that he is well on the way to recovery. They speak of a period of four weeks by the end of which he will probably be completely restored to health.' Schwind sounds as though trying to calm himself. He knew the truth.

On 9 December Johanna Lutz wrote to her fiancé Leopold Kupelwieser in Rome, 'Schubert is now quite well and already shows the inclination to stop keeping to his strict régime. If only he does not do himself harm.' She too knew more than she wrote. The doctor told Schubert to lead 'a regulated life' with plenty of exercise 'and no alcohol'. Just at a time when Schubert would have needed a glass of wine once in a while. On 26 December Schwind wrote to Schober, 'Schubert is better. It should not be long before he is able to wear his own hair again which he shaved off because of the rash. He is wearing a very nice wig.' The friends are trying hard to cheer each other up but they know about Schubert's sickness, and more details, such as the rash and the wig, emerge.

Apparently Schubert did not lead 'a regulated life'. On 13 February 1824 Schwind writes, 'Schubert is now keeping a fourteen-day fast and is confined to his house. He looks much better and is very cheerful and comically hungry. He writes innumerable quartets and Variations.' On 22 February Schwind informs Schober, 'Schubert is fine. He has abandoned his wig and is growing sweet little curls.' And a few days later, on 6 March, 'Schubert is now much

opposite A view of Graz, which Schubert visited in 1825, and where Anselm Hüttenbrenner was musical director.

better. He says that after a few days of the new treatment he felt that the back of the illness had been broken, that everything was different.'

Nothing but vague hints but Schubert did not tell much to his friends. What new treatment? Schwind tries to convince himself that Schubert is 'better'. Men are often helpless when facing sickness and death, and Schubert's friends were no exception. They were grateful for every bit of good news but they were not fooling themselves. Schubert put up a brave front and pretended to be cheerful when they visited him. It worried him to see them worry about him. But on 31 March he wrote the truth to Kupelwieser, who was far away in Rome, and to whom 'he could at last pour out his whole soul once more'.

I feel myself to be the unhappiest, most miserable being in the world. Imagine a man whose health will never be right again, and who in despair makes things worse and worse instead of better. Imagine a man whose brightest hopes have been shattered, to whom the happiness of love and friendship offers at best pain, whose enthusiasm (at least the stimulating kind) for beauty threatens to vanish: and then ask yourself if this is not an unhappy, miserable man? 'My peace is gone, my heart is heavy, and I shall find it never and nevermore.' Thus indeed I can now sing every day, for each night when I go to sleep I hope I will not wake again, and each morning reminds me of yesterday's unhappiness. Thus, joyless and friendless, I would pass my days, if Schwind didn't visit me occasionally and bring me a breath of those sweet days that are past ...

A shattering document that should destroy once and for all the legend of Schubert, the happy-go-lucky bohemian, the cheerful Biedermeier character. It shows the real Schubert – desperate and sorry for himself but also realistic and quietly convinced that nothing, nobody can help him anymore. If he could only go to sleep 'and not wake again'. To die painlessly, almost happily. The letter was written in a moment of deep depression but it reveals the bitter truth. Today the character of his sickness is no longer a matter of speculation, of trying not to mention the unmentionable. 'There is no doubt that it was venereal, probably syphilis,' concludes Professor O. E. Deutsch.

At that time no effective method of treatment existed. Schubert was doomed and he knew it. On 24 April the faithful Schwind wrote to Schober, 'Schubert is not very well. He has such pains in his left arm that he is quite unable to play the piano.'

And during all these months the 'unhappy, miserable man' wrote glorious music. His genius seems to have overcome illness and despair. When he wrote music he was in heaven. Perhaps this was what Johann Michael Vogl had meant when he talked of 'Schubert's somnambulistic state whenever he wrote music'.

On 25 March 1824 the official *Wiener Zeitung* had announced the publication of *Die schöne Müllerin*, 'a cycle of songs with text by Wilhelm Müller and set to music for solo voice with piano accompaniment, dedicated to Karl Freiherr von Schönstein, Opus 25'. A charming story survived about how Schubert discovered the poems of *Die schöne Müllerin*. One day he came to call on his old school friend Benedikt Randhartinger who was then the private secretary of Count Széchényi. After a moment Randhartinger was called away and left Schubert alone in his room. A book of poems was on Randhartinger's desk. Schubert was not surprised; he and his friends were always reading poetry. He began to read the poems, became interested, and there may have been the faraway look in his eyes that his friends knew well: Schubert was already singing in his mind. He put the book in his pocket and left the room.

Randhartinger returned and noticed that Schubert and the book of poetry were gone. Unfortunately it was not his book, it belonged to Count Széchényi. Randhartinger was worried, went to see Schubert, and asked him to return the book. According to the story Schubert did return it a few days later, 'but by that time he had written the whole cycle of songs'. The legend is irrelevant. *Die schöne Müllerin* remains one of Schubert's immortal masterpieces, truly a gift from God, greater in its entirety than in its components. Some *Lieder* that Schubert wrote may be finer, more beautiful – here we approach the subjective problem of taste and personal likes – but as a cycle *Die schöne Müllerin* is irresistible in its charm, variety, beauty. The words of the poem may suffer from sentimentality or a certain homespun simplicity. Müller was certainly no Goethe. But Schubert turned Müller's second-rate poetry into first-rate art. Many people feel that *Die schöne Müllerin*, the song cycle created during some of Schubert's unhappiest days, is sheer magic. It is pointless to write about the cycle. One has to hear it to enjoy it.

In the summer Schubert went back to Zseliz. On 21 September he wrote to the friends that he had been in good health 'for five months'. But they knew this was untrue. At the end of the year he had a relapse and was unable to attend his friends' New Year's party. He would have loved to be there but he was too ill. He was suffering from blinding headaches. He wrote on the manuscript of a march he had composed for the little son of his friend, Marie Leopoldine Pachler, 'I hope you are in better health than I am, Madame, for my usual headaches have started to attack me again.' It is one of the relatively few references to his health. Characteristically, it is written to Frau Pachler, not one of his close friends. Frau Pachler's house in Graz was the centre of the city's musical life. She played the piano very well. Beethoven once said, 'I've known no one who plays my compositions so well, not excepting the great pianists.' Schubert felt happy in her house when his health improved, and improvised dances and melodies during the *Schubertiaden* in her home. Her husband, a lawyer and beer brewer, was very interested in the local theatre.

At that time the friends in Vienna noticed that Schubert no longer seemed to take special care of himself. When they told him to go home and rest or to stop drinking wine, he would give a shrug. The friends thought he was courageous. He knew there was no hope for him, sooner or later he was going to die, and he was trying to enjoy what time there was left. There were good days and bad days but basically his condition remained unchanged. He would join his friends at the Heuriger gardens and in the coffee-houses of the Inner City, but sometimes he left a party early when there was too much *Würstel* eating and drinking; he said he was getting tired.

He was not tired though when he wrote his beloved music; he continued to compose at a fantastic pace. He read a great deal of poetry, always search-

below The town of Gmunden, which Schubert visited in 1825.

ing for something that might appeal to his 'enthusiasm for beauty' and stimulate his imagination. He read and composed the poems of his friends – Mayrhofer, Senn, Schober, Bruchmann and others – and discovered the lyric poetry of Friedrich Rückert and the fine poems of the classicist, Graf Platen. And he always returned to Goethe to compose *Lieder* that are among the best he left, *An die Entfernte*, *Der Musensohn* and *Wanderers Nachtlied* ('Über allen Gipfeln ist Ruh'), possibly the greatest poem Goethe ever wrote, incredibly simple, beautiful, true.

When his health was better Schubert moved around a little seeing his friends, trying to forget momentarily. He went to visit Anselm Hüttenbrenner who had become musical director in Graz, the capital of Styria, and to Linz in Upper Austria, Spaun's hometown. Late in May 1825 he went to see J. M. Vogl who lived after his retirement in Steyr and they went on 'a musical tour' to Linz, Gmunden, Salzburg and Gastein. Vogl sang Schubert *Lieder* and was accompanied by the composer at the piano. Schubert visited the monastery of St Florian in Upper Austria, where later Anton Bruckner was organist and now lies buried. Schubert wrote that he found Gmunden 'very pleasant'. He may have started work there on the so-called Gmunden-Gastein or Gastein Symphony which seems lost, one of the major riddles of Schubert's life. On 12 September 1825 Schubert wrote to his brother Ferdinand:

... Vogl sang some songs of mine, whereupon we were invited for the following evening and asked to do our stuff before a select assembly. The music made a great impression, especially the *Ave Maria*, mentioned in my earlier letter. The way in which Vogl sings and I accompany him, so that at such moments we seem to be *one*, is something quite new and unprecedented for these people ...

Golden words for generations of singers who attempt Schubert's *Lieder*, and the composer's unequivocal command of how his songs should be performed: so that singer and accompanist seem to be one. It sounds easy but is one of the hardest things to achieve.

Music was much on Schubert's mind although he had other interests as well. A few days later, on 21 September, he wrote to Ferdinand a long letter with his impressions of 'the extremely dirty and disgusting town of Hallein', and the 'wild scenery' he saw on the way to Gastein that reminded him of the war of 1809:

... It was here that the Bavarians were on one side of the Salzach, which forges its way far below; and the Tyroleans on the other, among the rocky peaks, fired down with devilish glee on the Bavarians who were trying to capture the pass. Those who were hit hurtled down into the depths without ever knowing where the shots had come from. This most shameful beginning which was continued for several days

The house at
Orth, Gmunden.

and weeks, is commemorated by a chapel on the Bavarian side and a red cross in the cliffs on the Tyrolean side, partly to mark the spot and partly, through these sacred symbols, as an atonement. Thou glorious Christ! To what abominations must Thou lend Thine image!!

In his last years Schubert wrote two works for violin and piano for his friend Karl Maria von Bocklet, the excellent pianist, and the young violinist Josef Slawik, sometimes spelled Slawjk. (An early Polonaise in B major, for violin and orchestra, written in 1817 for his brother Ferdinand, who played the solo part, was only published in 1928, D. 850.) The late works are different. The Rondo Op. 70 – Schubert called it *Rondeau brilliant* – was first performed at the home of Domenico Artaria early in 1827 and later published by him. This difficult piece demands great technical skill – some people called Slawik 'a new Paganini' – but it lacks the magic of Schubert who was never at his best when he wrote technically difficult virtuoso pieces. The second work was the Duo in C major Op. 159. Again some critics missed 'the real Schubert', which proves that they were beginning to understand the composer. *Der Sammler* noted that the piece 'lasts rather longer than the time the Viennese are prepared to devote to their aesthetic pleasures' and that consequently 'the hall gradually emptied'. We ought to be glad that audiences are better mannered now, even when they are bored.

The critic of the Leipzig *Allgemeine musikalische Zeitung* wrote, 'A new fantasia made no appeal of any sort. It would be fair judgement to say that the popular composer has gone off the rails here.' For once the critic seems to have been right. But a few months later Schubert, as unpredictable as ever, wrote the two Piano Trios Op. 99 and Op. 100. They are among his greatest chamber music works. Again Schumann was among the first who understood them.

One glance at Schubert's Trio Op. 99 and all the troubles of human existence disappear, and all the world is fresh and bright again ... To sum up, the Trio in E flat major (Op. 100) is active, masculine, dramatic, while the one in B flat major (Op. 99) is passive, feminine, lyrical.

Early in 1828 – the year of his death – Schubert was in relatively good health. Locally he was well known at last. Beethoven was dead and Schubert was the leading Viennese composer, the 'romanticist of classicism'. In his humble, realistic moments he knew that he was merely carrying on the heritage of Beethoven. But he still had much difficulty to find publishers for his 'serious' works, the symphonies and the chamber music. Beethoven had had no such problem. Practically everything he wrote was published. Sometimes different publishers competed for his work.

opposite The Ursuline Church at Salzburg.

overleaf A view of Linz.

Schubert's friends had for years encouraged him to give a public recital of his works, in the manner of Beethoven. In 1825 he and Leopold Kupelwieser had talked about it and in 1827 Bauernfeld wrote to Schubert:

opposite Leopoldskron House in Salzburg.

Everybody talks about you, and each of your songs is an event. You've composed magnificent string quartets and trios, not to mention your symphonies! Your friends love your works but no publisher wants to buy them, and the public has no idea of their beauty and grace. Make a start, get over your laziness, give a concert – only your things, of course. Vogl will gladly assist you and Bocklet, Böhm and Linke will be honoured to work for a master like you. People will fight for tickets, and though you may not become a Croesus, the one evening will see you through a whole year. Such an evening could be repeated every year, and if there is excitement – and there will be – you can put the pressure on the Diabellis, Artarias, and Haslingers with their shabby fees. A concert, listen to my advice, a concert!

The 'Private Concert' eventually took place, after Schubert had hesitated for a long time, at the Musikverein Hall at Tuchlauben 558 on 26 March, exactly one year after the day Beethoven had died. It was Schubert's first and last public concert and the programme consisted only of the works of Schubert. It was arranged in the manner of the former Beethoven concerts.

Schubert selected the pieces carefully. He tried to give the public some of what he considered his best works and some he hoped that might 'please'. The concert began with the first movement from his G major String Quartet. It is a long movement and Schubert was afraid to put the whole work on the programme. Joseph Böhm and three members of the Schuppanzigh Quartet – Holz, Weiss and Linke – performed it. J. M. Vogl sang *Der Kreuzzug, Die Sterne, Der Wanderer, An den Mond* and *Fragment from Aischylos*. This was followed by Grillparzer's *Ständchen*, the Piano Trio in E flat major, and more songs, again performed by Vogl and Ludwig Tietze, a noted amateur tenor and Schubert enthusiast. The concert ended with Klopstock's *Schlachtgesang*, performed by a male chorus.

Bauernfeld who had done so much to encourage Schubert noted in his diary, 'Terrific applause. The hall was crowded, every piece was cheered, the composer was called again and again. The net proceeds were almost 800 florins.' Another friend, Franz von Hartmann, wrote, 'With Louis and Enk at Schubert's concert. I'll never forget how beautiful it was. At the Schnecke we celebrated until midnight.'

Yet the success of the 'Private Concert' was more private than public. The local newspapers ignored the event. Very late, on 2 July, the *Berliner Allgemeine Musikalische Zeitung* wrote that 'the numerous friends and protectors applauded enthusiastically and several numbers were repeated'. In Vienna Schubert was not yet known as a great composer. However he was still the much-liked 'compositeur' of *Lieder*. He spent some of his money buying a piano – until then he had rented one – and paying off his debts. A few days later he invited Bauernfeld to hear Niccolò Paganini at the Imperial Ballrooms (today's Redoutensäle) at the Hofburg. The least expensive ticket was five florins – five times the usual price – and the five-guilder notes became known as 'Paganiners'.

Forty-one years later, in 1869, Bauernfeld remembered:

Schubert said, 'I've already heard him once, I tell you, we shall never see this fellow's likes again! And I have lots of money now. Come on!' Who could have resisted such an appeal? So we heard the diabolically sublime violinist, on whose flights of imagination Heine's own imagination plays so beautifully, and our delight over his wonderful Adagio was no less great that our utter amazement at the rest of his devilish tricks. We also derived no little amazement from the incredible bows of the demoniac figure who resembled a thin, black puppet operated by wires. According to the custom I was also treated at the inn after the concert, and a bottle more than usual was charged up to enthusiasm.

Jngres Del.
Roma 1819.

It was Paganini's first tour outside of Italy; he was then forty-four. He had met Prince Metternich in Rome and was invited to come to Vienna where he gave twenty concerts. He played almost exclusively his own compositions, his Violin Concerto No. 1, his Variations on *Non più andrai* from Mozart's *Figaro*, and his Variations on an Aria from Rossini's *Cenerentola*. The critics were unable to adequately express their enthusiasm; words failed them, which happened rarely in Vienna. Schubert left 'as in trance'. Many other composers had similar feelings when they heard Paganini. Chopin was 'completely overcome with emotion'. Schumann said that Paganini's compositions contained 'the purest, most valuable qualities'. Schubert's romantic soul sensed a deep affinity with the great romantic of the violin. After the Adagio of Paganini's Concerto No. 2 Schubert said that he had heard 'an angel singing in it'.

Schubert's last year was a year of enormous productivity, as though God wanted to bless him once more. He wrote the String Quintet, the Fantasy in F minor for piano duet, his last three piano sonatas, thirteen songs published one year after his death by Haslinger under the title *Schwanengesang* (Swan Song), the great choral work *Miriams Siegesgesang* (Miriam's Song of Triumph) after a text by Grillparzer, and his great Mass in E flat major. And he wrote the C major Symphony, which is now called The Great to distinguish it from his earlier Little C major Symphony No. 6. Schumann wrote, 'He who has not heard the C major Symphony doesn't really know Schubert.'

Schubert heard some of these works performed and some he played himself. The F minor Piano Fantasy for four hands was intended for Countess Caroline Esterházy, as we know from one of Schubert's letters to Schott, the publisher in Mainz. Schubert played it with Lachner for their friend Bauernfeld on 9 May. It is among his finest piano compositions. Schott turned it down. It was published after Schubert's death by Diabelli in Vienna. Equally sad is the history of the String Quintet which he wrote in August and September. This masterpiece has no equal in the whole literature. Some, like Alfred Einstein, believe Schubert may have written it because 'he had no longer cause to fear the critical presence of Beethoven'. But Schubert never wrote anything for a negative reason; he wrote the Quintet because he felt he had to write it. It may be superficially close to Beethoven, with its powerful structure but it is completely Schubertian nevertheless. It is orchestral, rather than strictly chamber, music but that was the way Schubert wrote towards the end of his life. In the exuberant Scherzo he seems to glorify the Austrian landscape – somewhat as Bruckner did later in his symphonies – and the Andante is sombre and lyrical and makes one think of death. The C major String Quintet is a greater work of art than the Great C major Symphony which he wrote a few months earlier. With only five voices – Schubert uses a second cello that is treated differently from the first – he expressed a whole musical universe. A very great work.

It was performed for the first time twenty-two years after the death of Schubert, on 7 November 1850 at the Musikverein Hall by Joseph Hellmesberger's String Quartet. Hellmesberger, born in 1828, the year Schubert died, late did much to rediscover him. His father had been a fellow chorister and schoolmate of Schubert. Three years after the Hellmesberger performance the String Quintet was published by Spina in Vienna.

Towards the end of his life Schubert wrote some of his greatest chamber musical and orchestral works. He knew there was no hope of the Octet, the String Quintet and the String Quartet in G major being published. His manuscript remained in the vault of the music publisher Diabelli for twenty years before some of them were first performed and then published.

Schubert knew he was soon going to die but he went on with his work. The 'cheerful little man' had enormous resources of will power. Late in his last summer, 1828, he finished what is now known as the Great C major Symphony. After his death no one bothered to look for it until Robert Schumann came to Vienna in the autumn of 1838.

Between his great symphony and the very great String Quintet Schubert found time, in June and July, to write his greatest Mass, in E flat major. We do not know what made him write such a large work. Perhaps he still hoped in a forlorn way for some kind of official appointment. Salieri had died in 1826 and his deputy Joseph Eybler had succeeded him as Chief Court Director of Music. Schubert applied for the post of deputy conductor and was turned down. Instead Joseph Weigl, Eybler's former assistant and a popular composer of operas, was appointed. Schubert never succeeded with any application in his life. He never bothered to meet and impress the 'right' people. Vienna's bureaucrats were no more perceptive than bureaucrats elsewhere. Herr Schubert was just another 'compositeur' of popular songs. There is great music in the Mass in E flat major. It was heard only once. Schubert's brother Ferdinand arranged a performance at the parish church of Mary the Comforter on 15 November 1829, once year after Schubert's death. Thereafter the Mass was ignored.

In September Schubert's health deteriorated. The Court physician Dr Ernst Rinna suggested that he move out of the Inner City. He was then staying with Schober. Dr Rinna thought 'the air was better' in the suburbs. Schubert moved once more, to the apartment of his brother Ferdinand at

Direktor der k. k. Normalhaupt- u. Unterrealschule bei
St. Anna in Wien, Inhaber des goldenen Verdienst-
kreuzes mit der Krone.

the Neue Wieden suburb, Firmiansgasse 694, 'second floor right'. (It is now Kettenbrückengasse 6, in Vienna's fourth district.)

It was a new house, still wet, not very good for a sick man. Schubert, more sensitive than ever, sensed there was not much time left. He wanted to be with his favourite brother. He had read the English edition of the works of Handel and thought he might 'seriously study counterpoint'. He contacted Simon Sechter, the noted court organist who twenty-five years later was the teacher of Anton Bruckner. At the beginning of November Schubert had a long lesson with Sechter – the first and the last. A few weeks earlier he had suddenly felt better and had walked in Eisenstadt with Ferdinand and some other people. On 2 October he had been well enough to write two letters to the publishers. In one letter, to Schott, he inquired about some manuscripts he had sent there. To Probst he wrote about his new Quintet for two violins, viola and two cellos 'which will be rehearsed one of these days'. He was finally trying to get his works published and better known, but it was too late. Schott replied haggling about money. 'It seems an error that we should pay 60 florins.' They turned down the piano work Op. 101 'because its unusability in France was disappointing. If you have occasionally something less difficult yet brilliant, in a less complicated key, we ask you to send us such a work.' The old story; they wanted the popular material that sells easily.

There were small consolations though. Schubert had sent the 23rd Psalm to the Women's Caecilia Verein in Lemberg (today Lwów) in Galicia which then belonged to Austria. He had written the Psalm back in 1820 for a musical soirée of Anna Fröhlich's pupils at the Conservatory of the Musikfreunde. It is a beautiful work for two sopranos and two contraltos with piano accompaniment. The conductor in Lemberg, Franz Xaver Wolfgang Mozart who was Mozart's second son, had asked Schubert's friend Spaun to thank Schubert on his behalf. In his Reminiscences Spaun remembered:

Schubert had told me to make a copy of the Grillparzer *Ständchen* and to send it to the ladies in Lemberg. I made the copy and took it to Schubert so he could correct it. I found him sick in bed but his condition seemed not serious to me. He corrected the copy, was glad to see me, and said, 'I've got all I need, but I am so weak that I feel like falling through my bed.'

Spaun left apparently convinced that Schubert's condition was no worse than so often before. But Schubert was so miserable that he overcame his customary reticence and wrote to Schober:

I am ill. For the last eleven days I have had nothing to eat or drink. I can only walk feebly from my armchair to my bed and back. Dr Rinna is treating me. Whenever I take any food I cannot manage to keep it. Please be so kind and let me have

opposite Schubert's brother Ferdinand, in whose house he lived from September 1898 until his death.

some books in this desperate plight. Those of [Fenimore] Cooper's I have read are *The Last of the Mohicans*, *The Spy*, *The Pilot* and *The Pioneers*. If by any chance you have anything else by him I beg you to leave it for me with Frau von Bogner at the coffeehouse. My brother, who is very conscientious will be the most reliable person to bring it to me. Or something else instead ...

It was his last letter. There was no date on it, as was Schubert's custom, but Schober wrote on it, 'Received 12 November 1828'. He did not go and see Schubert. Schubert was said to have 'nervous fever' and Schober may have been afraid to be infected, which was not unreasonable because it happened often. Anything that puzzled the doctors in those days, from typhoid to depressions, was 'nervous fever'.

Shortly before his death Schubert wanted to hear Beethoven's C sharp minor Quartet Op. 131, perhaps Beethoven's greatest quartet. It had been published the year before and had not been publicly performed. Karl Holz, the violinist who had played at Schubert's 'Private Concert', arranged a special performance. Did Schubert want to hear Beethoven's 'sounds of the future' because he sensed prophetic aspects in his own music? Or was he just interested in another Beethoven masterpiece? According to Deutsch the private recital took place on 14 November. Holz later stated that 'in five days Schubert was dead'. Schubert was said to be deeply moved and it was feared that the performance may have worsened his condition. It is hard to accept the fact that Schubert left his home in his feeble condition. Perhaps he heard Beethoven's masterpiece earlier; but when he did he was certainly deeply impressed by it. He well understood its mystical greatness.

On 17 November, a Monday, Bauernfeld and Franz Lachner came to visit their sick friend. Schubert was lying with his face to the wall 'in a delirious fever'. In their subsequent accounts both Bauernfeld and Lachner agree that Schubert had a lucid interval in the afternoon and they talked with him about Bauernfeld's libretto *Der Graf von Gleichen*, which Schubert had liked for a long time and wanted to use for another opera. Bauernfeld's libretto is amusing but it deals with the problem of bigamy which was of course *verboten* by Metternich's censors. In his diary Bauernfeld remembers that at the end of July 1826 he returned from a holiday in the Salzkammergut and came to Nussdorf to meet Schubert and Schwind. They rushed out of a wine house and Schubert said, 'Where is the opera?' But the composer, so naïve and unworldly, must have had some second thoughts after all. On 26 August Bauernfeld noted, 'Schubert is delighted with the opera but we are afraid of the censor.' Later he wrote, 'The opera libretto is forbidden by the censor. Schubert wants to compose it nevertheless.' And on 31 August Bauernfeld wrote in his dairy, 'Schubert is composing *Der Graf von Gleichen*.'

Beethoven, whom Schubert greatly admired. He heard a 'private concert' of the C sharp minor quartet shortly before his death.

Bauernfeld later said that Schubert had been working on the orchestration of the opera just before he died. Bauernfeld was mistaken, or his memory was getting unreliable. Forty years later Ludwig Herbeck wrote in the biography of his father, Johann Herbeck who was the first director of the Musikfreunde and after 1870 *Direktor* of the Vienna Court Opera, 'Schubert's manuscript of *Graf von Gleichen* came into Herbeck's (my father's) possession. It can really be described as nothing more than a sketch. Only the voice parts had been completed in detail.'

179

lasse, ob es Dir sehr gut geht, so wie deiner lieben Familie
und deinem Bruder. Grüße mir Alles auf's herz-
lichste. Neulich ist von mir ein Trio für Pianoforte,
Violin u. Violoncello bey Schuppanzigh aufgeführt wor-
den und hat sehr gefallen. Es wurde von Bocklet, Schuppanzigh u. Linke vortrefflich exekutirt. Hast du nicht Kun-
peinsch Apropos, wenn nochmal dann die 2 Linke
bey Hartmann oder wie es heißt, nicht? Wird ich denn
bald 2 Vexirmarsch spielen !!!

Ich wiederhole meine obige Bitt, u. wehe mir,
wirst du meinem Wunsch, schreibst Du mir.

In Erwartung einer angenehmen Nachricht
verbleibe ich
dein treuer Freund
bis in den Tod

Frz. Schubert m/p.

However Bauernfeld and Lachner did talk about the project the last time they saw Schubert, discussing 'with the most modest and sympathetic of friends' the problems of opera – the one musical form in which Schubert had never succeeded.

The following day, 18 November, Schubert called his brother Ferdinand and complained that he was kept 'in a strange room'. He was almost delirious. Ferdinand remembered, 'Though only half-conscious he said to me, "I implore you to transfer me to my room, not to leave me here, in this corner under the earth. Do I deserve no place above the earth?"'

Ferdinand told him that he was in his own bed. 'And Franz said, "No it is not true, Beethoven doesn't lie here."' Ferdinand wrote a detailed record of this conversation two days after his brother's death. He understood correctly his brother's last wish to be buried near Beethoven.

In his *Buddenbrooks* Thomas Mann writes at length about the symptoms of typhoid fever. Some people have ventured the opinion that Mann may have had Schubert in mind.

When the fever is at its height life calls to the patient, calls out to him as he wanders in his distant dream ... [There are the early symptoms] depression, weariness, lack of appetite, headache and unquiet sleep ... up to the third week, up to the very crisis of the disease, the doctor cannot possibly tell whether this illness which he calls typhoid is an unfortunate accident, the disagreeable consequence of an infection ... or whether it is, quite simply, a form of dissolution, the garment, as it were, of death ...

Schubert's sickness followed the three week rhythm of typhoid fever. The first week he felt tired and depressed but he was able to walk around and do some work. The second week his misery got worse and he wrote the depressed (and depressing) letter to Schober. Then came the third and final week of 'dissolution, the garment, as it were, of death ...'

Typhoid fever (abdominal typhus) was then endemic in Vienna. Schubert may have drunk infected water. It is also remembered that some time earlier he had eaten some bad fish at an inn and had complained of nausea. When he was lying there delirious he would sing softly. Dr Rinna came and tried to cheer up the patient – there was little else he could do. Schubert, perhaps in another lucid moment, shook his head and replied, 'Here, here is my end.' The last work he did before losing consciousness was to correct some proofs of the second part of the *Winterreise* cycle from Tobias Haslinger, the publisher. Haslinger published the *Lieder* a few weeks after Schubert's death.

On 19 November, a Wednesday, Schubert never regained consciousness. His feeble, sick body was unable to resist the infection. He died at three o'clock in the afternoon.

One of Schubert's last letters, to Anselm Hüttenbrenner.

'He has died in his greatness,' Schwind, then in Munich, wrote. 'The more I realize now what he was like, the more I see what he has suffered.' He also wrote what might have been a beautiful epitaph, 'Schubert is dead and with him all that we had of the brightest and fairest'. Bauernfeld wrote in his diary, 'I wish I lay there, in his place ... For he leaves the world with fame.'

The house in Kettenbrückengasse 6 where Schubert died looks now almost as it did when Schubert moved there in September 1828. He knew he was going to die and he wanted to be close to his favourite brother, Ferdinand. Except for a memorial tablet and two Austrian flags the house is not different from others in the vicinity in the style of the era – more attractive than the pompous horrors that were put up in the district towards the end of the century, and the functional horrors that are now being built there. The district seems unable to make up its mind whether to preserve some memories of the past or to forget the past altogether and become 'modern'. The

The house in which Schubert died.

Schubert house is no shrine. A large store with several shop windows occupies the ground floor. Through the entrance one reaches a square courtyard around which the house was built. The well was in one corner and the tenants had to go there for water. Now the site of the well is covered by a flower arrangement. The tenants get their water from the *bassena* (from the French *bassin*) on each corridor. Vienna still has many such *bassena* houses with a minimum of plumbing and community toilets on the floor.

Ferdinand Schubert and his large family – he had thirteen children at that time – occupied the entire third floor (in Vienna it is known as the second floor) and a stairway of stone leads up there. There is a smell of dust and mortar. Ferdinand was then a person of some importance, working at the Normal-Hauptschule of St Anna, a teacher training college. Later on he became Principal of the school. He was perhaps widely envied for the large new apartment into which the family had recently moved. Franz Schubert was given a small room, hardly larger than a modern prison cell, with one window looking out on to the street. The room has a tiny anteroom and a separate entrance from the corridor. (According to some local sources, Schubert did not die in the room looking out on to the street, but in a smaller room with a tiny window facing the courtyard. Officially though, the room facing the street is the one where he is said to have died on November 19.) There is no furniture of historical importance. The few pieces that were there when Schubert died – his bed, a couple of chairs, a small table – have disappeared and the City of Vienna sensibly refused to put some false memorial antiques there. Only the brightly scrubbed wooden floorboards, on which Schubert walked, have remained. It is a depressingly poor place. Schubert was born poor and he died poor.

A few framed pictures and documents hang on the walls and other memorabilia are shown in two glass cases: the death certificate giving Schubert's profession as *Tonkünstler und Compositeur*; the printed announcement of his death and of the memorial Mass at which Mozart's *Requiem* was performed; his last letter to Schober; the first part of Haslinger's first edition of *Winterreise* that had been published in January 1828 (the second part which Schubert corrected in this room was published a few weeks after his death, late in December); the text of Franz Grillparzer's famous epitaph; and a copy of Cooper's *Der Lootse*, possibly the last book Schubert read.

Franz Schubert was given a second-class funeral for which his father paid. At the funeral service a Schubert poem was sung in church with the music taken from his *Pax vobiscum*. It contains some lines proving that his brother Ferdinand, in charge of the service, had truly understood Schubert:

For many roses did this life on earth
With pointed thorns reward thee for thy worth,
With pain and sorrow and an early grave.

His 'early grave' was not in the cemetery belonging to the Wieden suburb but on the other side of Vienna in the Währing Cemetery, three graves away from Beethoven. Schubert's last wish was fulfilled. The former cemetery is now the Schubert Park. The monuments of Beethoven and Schubert are still there. On the flat architrave above Schubert's grave there was the inscription written by Grillparzer:

DIE TONKUNST BEGRUB HIER EINEN REICHEN BESITZ

ABER NOCH VIEL SCHÖNERE HOFFNUNGEN

FRANZ SCHUBERT LIEGT HIER

GEBOREN AM XXXI JANUAR MDCCXCVII

GESTORBEN AM XIX NOVEMBER MDCCCXXVIII

XXXI JAHRE ALT

'The art of music here interred a rich possession/But far fairer hopes still' is basically true, but not the implication that Schubert's work was left incomplete. In 1888 the remains of Beethoven and Schubert were transferred to Graves of Honour at the Central Cemetery. At Schubert's grave there is the tombstone made by the sculptor Karl Kundmann.

The receipted bill for the funeral expenses, from the undertaker Balthasar Ausim, is kept in the Archives of the City of Vienna. Schubert's funeral was more expensive than Mozart's; in the case of Schubert we know at least where he is buried. Still, the comparison between the two poor (and very rich) composers is interesting. Schubert's funeral Mass was celebrated at the Wieden parish church and the tax paid was twenty florins and twenty-seven kreuzer, compared with the fee paid to St Stephen's for the last rites of Mozart, only eight florins and fifty-six kreuzer. Schubert's father and his brothers wanted Franz to have 'a nice funeral' with singing and organ playing, wreaths, a painted coffin, a fine shroud, candles, printed announcements of his death, mourning cloaks, a Cross, praying in vigil, tips and other expenses. How Schubert himself might have felt about the ceremonial is beside the point. Funerals were always important in Vienna; they still are and a *schöne Leich* (a nice funeral) is widely appreciated, especially by those who do not know the deceased. There were expenses to be paid at the Währing Cemetery, thirty florins for the individual grave. (No such expenses were paid at the St Mark's Cemetery where some thirty years earlier Mozart had been dumped in a narrow grave with some dozen strangers.)

opposite The tavern 'Zum Heurigen' in Grinzing.

overleaf The confluence of the rivers Enns and Steyr in upper Austria, which Schubert visited in the last year of his life.

184

Schubert's finances at the time of his death were as confused as during most of his life. When he moved to Ferdinand's flat he had on him 118 florins. Most of the money went on doctor's expenses and medicines. He paid a little money to Ferdinand for room and board. At his death he owed money to Schober, two tailors, a shoemaker, a pianoforte maker for repairs on Schober's piano, and to others.

The family paid all his debts. Ferdinand acted as treasurer and later gave his father a detailed account. After Schubert's death Ferdinand was offered seventy florins by the publisher Haslinger for each of the last three piano sonatas. One year after Schubert's death, in November 1829, Ferdinand made an agreement with the publisher Diabelli who paid 2400 florins for many songs, piano pieces and 'music for string instruments'. (Beethoven left 9000 gulden to his nephew Karl.) Did Diabelli truly understand what treasures he had bought? If he did, he did nothing about it. Many of the great works remained in Diabelli's vault. Some remained with Diabelli's successor, the music publisher Spina, until the 1870s, almost half a century after Schubert's death. In the case of Schubert the music publishers in Vienna and Germany showed themselves utterly incompetent, petty and narrow-minded.

Schubert had never cared about success or money. His lack of self-assurance and his shyness were later attributed to his strict upbringing, the joyless years at the Stadtkonvikt, possibly his short stature and early profession as his father's assistant. Later he was often upset about the failures of his operas but he rarely complained. He knew no personal vanity. One evening when one of his works was on the programme of a public concert, which was not a regular occurrence, Schubert ignored the event and went to see a play by Grillparzer. But he knew his value. He was not pleased when his brother Ferdinand told him that the musical clock at the Hotel Ungarische Krone ran cylinders with some of Schubert's waltzes. He would have been more pleased had Ferdinand told him something nice about his chamber music.

The estimated value of Schubert's total assets at his death was exactly sixty-three florins. It was made up of the following items:

3 cloth dress coats, 3 frock coats, 10 pairs of trousers, and 9 waistcoats	37 fl.
1 hat, 5 pairs of shoes, 2 pairs of boots	2 fl.
4 shirts, 9 neck- and hand-kerchiefs, 13 pairs of socks, 1 sheet, 2 blanket cases	8 fl.
1 mattress, 1 pillow, 1 blanket	6 fl.
Some old music, valued at	10 fl.

previous page Gmunden in upper Austria, a favourite holiday place of Schubert's.

opposite Watercolour of Schubert.

The printed sequestration report does not say whether 'some old music' contained any Schubert manuscripts. Sixty-three florins! What is the value of the A minor Quartet, the *Unfinished* Symphony, the cycles *Die schöne Müllerin* and *Winterreise*, of *Heidenröslein* and *Erlkönig*? It is indeed a report on human stupidity. Genius always remains misunderstood.

The report contained the question whether there were any books among the property, and whether a report concerning them had been made to the Kaiser-Königlich Book Revision Office immediately after sequestration. Metternich's censorship was very tight. No books were listed among the property. But Schubert had always had books, he loved to be surrounded by books. It is assumed he left most of them at Schober's house or that his brother Ferdinand had them quickly removed.

In the 1830s the death rate from typhus, dysentery and pulmonary tuberculosis was very high and Vienna had a population deficit of about 8 per cent. Under such conditions Schubert's 'early grave' was perhaps not as unusual as we might think.

We already know that few of Schubert's works were published at the time of his death. The list is pitifully small. None of his symphonies, no stage work, only two piano sonatas, one string quartet out of fourteen, no other chamber music, no church music and only about 200 *Lieder*. 'Of Schubert's *Lieder* too many are still unknown,' wrote Fischer-Dieskau in 1974, and he lists five solo songs that will be published in Bärenreiter's new Complete Edition: *Jägers Abendlied* (1815, Goethe), *Am ersten Maimorgen* (1816, Claudius), *Mailied* (1816, Hölty), *Lebensmut* (1828, Leitner) and one untitled *Lied*, 1817.

By 1830 Schubert's name was rarely mentioned except by his friends and close relatives. There had been several concerts to collect funds for a monument and now the monument was finished. On 18 November 1830 Heinrich Heine wrote to Eduard Marxsen in Vienna (who became the teacher of Brahms) 'Schubart (*sic*) is said to have set very good music to my poems shortly before his death. Unfortunately I don't know them.' Among the 'very good music' are three masterpieces, now much admired; *Schwanengesang*: *Am Meer*, *Die Stadt*, and *Der Doppelgänger*. When Schubert died hundreds of *Lieder* were kept in a box in Ferdinand's apartment and other songs were scattered among his friends. 'Much was lost and other things were acquired by national and state libraries,' writes Fischer-Dieskau.

Six years after Schubert's death the noted music historian Raphael Georg Kiesewetter, who had known Schubert and his friends, wrote about the recent period in his *History of European-Occidental Music* in the chapter *The Epoch of Beethoven and Rossini*. He never mentioned Schubert.

opposite The courtyard of the house in which Schubert died in 1828.

191

The invitation issued by Schubert's father to his funeral on 23 December 1828.

But Schubert was not forgotten, even though he was not popular then. Spaun remembers *die herrlichen Lieder* (the wonderful songs) that were sung by Vogl and Schönstein and 'caused mounting enthusiasm'. A few days before his death in 1843 J.M. Vogl sang *Winterreise* at the home of *Hofrat* Enderes. It was Vogl's last appearance. Spaun writes that 'everybody was deeply moved ... Few are still alive who remember Vogl's singing. They haven't heard anything similar since.'

In the spring of 1838 Franz Liszt began performing his brilliant paraphrases of Schubert's songs and dance tunes. Liszt arranged them for virtuoso performances on the piano; often he played the melody with the left hand as though it were sung by a baritone, and later he would change to the right hand. He took other liberties and outraged purists quickly called his transcriptions 'sacrilegious'. Liszt was a romantic who loved romantic sounds. He called Schubert 'the most poetic musician' of all and once said, 'In the short time it takes to sing a *Lied* Schubert turns us into spectators of fast, fateful conflicts.' An astute statement, proving that Liszt (like Robert Schumann) thoroughly understood the phenomenon of Franz Schubert that was then still widely unknown.

There is no text in Liszt's transcriptions of Schubert's *Lieder* but Schubert's imagination gloriously survives. Liszt worked with devotion and artistic understanding, turning some *Lieder* into minor symphonic poems. His first collection, published by Haslinger in 1838, was called *Hommage aux Dames de Vienne* and contained *Ständchen*, *Lob der Tränen*, *Die Post*, and *Die Rose*. The title seems somewhat old-fashioned and so is a later title *Soirées de Vienne*, but Liszt, the virtuoso performer, knew what his public wanted. Eventually he published some sixty Schubert songs and played them everywhere for people who had never heard Schubert's original *Lieder*. There was a certain danger that the original composer, not yet too well established, might lose his identity behind the powerful, present image of the great performer and transcriber, but Liszt avoided the danger by his reverence and enthusiasm for Schubert.

Franz Liszt.

Liszt was attracted by some of Schubert's most powerful songs. He transcribed among others *Du bist die Ruh'*, *Erlkönig*, *Rastlose Liebe*, *Ungeduld*, *Die Forelle*, *Die Taubenpost*, *Der Lindenbaum*, and *Der Leiermann*. He paraphrased four songs for orchestra – *Die junge Nonne*, *Gretchen am Spinnrade*, *Lied der Mignon*, *Erlkönig* – and in 1870 in Budapest he transcribed Schubert's *Die Allmacht* for tenor, men's chorus and orchestra.

Probably Schubert would not have criticized Liszt if he had watched the large audiences that were deeply moved by these transcriptions. A critic in Leipzig wrote that 'Liszt made the piano sing out as no one before him'. Exactly what Schubert would have done if he had had Liszt's technique.

Occasionally a long forgotten Schubert work is rediscovered and performed. Several years ago Hans Petermandl, the noted pianist from Linz, found a piano piece among the manuscripts once kept in Graz by Anselm Hüttenbrenner. The so-called Graz Fantasy was performed and published. Today Schubert would have no problems having his manuscripts published. In June 1976 in Vienna the pianist Jörg Demus performed a Schubert Fantasy in C minor, now listed in the Deutsch Catalogue as D. 993. It seems to be an early work, written in 1813. Schubert was then sixteen and he used two motifs from Mozart's C minor Fantasy K.475, perhaps to show his admiration for Mozart.

Musicians are always hoping to find other genuine Schubert manuscripts. But the chances of finding one are perhaps as dim as the discovery of an old violin in the attic that turns out to be a genuine Stradivari.

The Finished Unfinished Symphony

Some people cannot help speculating what might have happened if Schubert had lived longer. Mozart died at the age of thirty-five. Suppose, they say, Mozart had only reached Schubert's age, thirty-one? We might have no *Cosi fan tutte*, no *La Clemenza di Tito*, no *Zauberflöte*, no *Requiem*. None of Mozart's great string quintets, no piano concertoes, no late symphonies. A disconcerting thought. Suppose, others say, Schubert had lived as long as Haydn or Verdi – seventy-seven and eighty-eight respectively? Haydn was sixty-seven when he wrote the *Seasons*. Verdi was nearly eighty when he wrote the youthful magic of *Falstaff*. Where was Beethoven at thirty-one? Before his Second Symphony.

Such speculation is naturally absurd. We should be thankful for having Schubert at all. His short, rich life gave us a whole new dimension in music. His *Lieder* created a new art form; they were never surpassed, only rarely attained. His greatest *Lieder* alone make Schubert immortal. And he gave us all the other treasures, his symphonies, his chamber music, the piano works and the Masses – so let us be properly grateful.

It is almost axiomatic that 'only Italians understand the mystery of the human voice'. Mozart wrote his great operas in Italian, treating even the orchestral 'voices' like vocal parts. Schubert never learned Italian and yet invented and perfected the magic of the *Lied*, the ideal communion of poem and sound, of image and music. Almost everything Schubert wrote was a sort of *Lied*. In his chamber music and in his symphonies the structure is often broken up by a song-like melody. This irritates the academics and theorists because 'it shouldn't be there'. But it makes musicians happy because the sudden, spontaneous intrusions are always beautiful. It may not be metronome music but it is melodious music. Schubert cannot be played with customary time-beating or bowing; many of his phrases can only be understood when one tries to sing them. They are always melodies that can be sung.

We simply cannot understand how Schubert divined the poetic elements

opposite The last page of the score of the B minor 'Unfinished' Symphony.

197

in a poem, how he sensed the music in the words. Almost no one after him did it as well, although many have tried. Good songs have been written by other composers. They are beautiful when sung by good singers but they never contain absolute ideas of musical images, the way Beethoven's last quartets are absolute music. Schubert's best songs are beautiful even without the text, just as Verdi in *Otello* and *Falstaff* makes you happy though you may not understand the words. Only great music can do that when it becomes an absolute force. The borderline between such music and merely very good music is sometimes hardly noticeable. Bruckner had a great affinity with Schubert and was close to him by environment, musical landscape and Austrian traditions. Yet he is very different. Occasionally Bruckner's repetitious length is not 'heavenly', it is just too long.

Schubert's *Unfinished* Symphony in B minor is now perhaps his best-loved symphonic work and one of the most frequently performed orchestral works. The popular belief that the *Unfinished* Symphony was incomplete is as wrong as the popular legend of 'Schwammerl'. Schubert never thought of the B minor Symphony as an unfinished work, a torso. It was given its name long after his death. The *Unfinished* Symphony is a fragment, but a complete one. It must not be compared to the genuine musical fragments – Bach's *Art of Fugue*, Mozart's *Requiem*, Bruckner's Ninth Symphony, Mahler's Tenth Symphony, works that remained uncompleted because the composer did not have the strength to finish them, or because death interfered. 'The cruel hand of Fate' is often evident in Schubert's short life, but certainly not in his *Unfinished* Symphony.

Schubert began working on the score of the B minor Symphony on 30 October 1822, as we know from the date he put down on the manuscript. That was six years before his death. The great work, profound and moving, that beautifully expresses the struggles of humanity was written by a young man of twenty-five who unhappily revered Beethoven, whose ancestry may sometimes be heard in this work. Some time in November the two movements were completed. Schubert made a rough sketch of a Scherzo that would follow. Then he put the manuscript of the symphony aside and finished the *Wanderer* Fantasy, an artful improvisation around his *Lied Der Wanderer*. Schubert knew that Mozart and Beethoven had often improvised in public; the art of writing musical variations was much respected. Schubert wrote masterful variations on his great *Lied* in the Adagio movement of the Fantasy.

In the spring of 1823 Schubert was made an Honorary Member of the Styrian Music Society in Graz. He was given a diploma by the Society's

The C minor quartet.

secretary. Schubert wrote a letter of thanks to the Society. 'In order to express my thanks in tones' he promised to send them 'the score of one of my symphonies'.

In September 1823 Schubert gave the score of the B minor Symphony to Josef Hüttenbrenner, whose brother Anselm was a member of the Styrian Music Society. The Hüttenbrenners belonged to the inner circle of Schubert's close friends. Now starts the mystery around the B minor Symphony. Josef kept the score for four years and only gave it to his brother in 1827. Why? The usual suggestion that he forgot is not convincing. Schubert's friends did not forget about one of his symphonies. And then Anselm Hüttenbrenner did not give the score to the Society, which had been Schubert's intention. He kept it at home with other Schubert manuscripts, among them

199

the operas *Des Teufels Lustschloss* and *Claudine von Villa Bella*. Again one asks, why?

Anselm Hüttenbrenner (1794–1868) was a good pianist, a mediocre composer, and something of a busybody who liked to be in the entourage of famous people. According to Schindler, Beethoven's first biographer, Anselm Hüttenbrenner was alone with Beethoven when Beethoven died and closed the great man's eyes. Schubert liked him. Hüttenbrenner had accompanied Vogl during the first public performance of *Erlkönig* in 1821 at the Kärntnertor Theater. But now the mystery deepens. Schubert never seems to have mentioned his B minor Symphony. His brother Ferdinand was unaware of it and does not mention it in his list of Schubert's works.

Nothing seems to have happened about the forgotten symphony until about 1850 when Josef Hüttenbrenner spoke about it to Kreissle who was collecting material for his first Schubert biography. Hüttenbrenner himself remembered that in 1860 he told Johann Herbeck, at that time conductor of the Society of Friends of Music, 'My brother (Anselm) possesses a treasure in Schubert's B minor Symphony which we place on a level with any of Beethoven's. Only it isn't finished. Schubert gave it to me for Anselm as thanks for having sent him, through me, the Diploma of Honour of the Graz Musical Society.'

Josef Hüttenbrenner's statement clears up some of the confusion. Apparently the brothers never intended to give the score to the Society. They kept it themselves and Anselm, who had become a bitter eccentric and lived a lonely life in Graz, kept his 'treasure' without showing it to anybody. He kept it for over forty years. He was an unsuccessful composer and it is hinted he may have been jealous of his old, dead friend Schubert, who was becoming very famous.

Johann Herbeck, a decent man and a good musician, did what he knew he must. He went to see Anselm Hüttenbrenner in Graz and talked to him. Apparently it was difficult to convince the old man that his 'treasure' belonged to the world. Eventually though he handed over the manuscript to Herbeck, but only after the conductor had promised Hüttenbrenner to perform one of his own orchestral works in Vienna. Herbeck kept his promise.

On 17 December 1865 Herbeck conducted the first performance of the *Unfinished* Symphony, forty-three years after Schubert had written it. Since the public might not appreciate a 'fragment', Herbeck added the finale from Schubert's earlier D major Symphony. When the *Unfinished* Symphony was performed in London in 1867 the Entr'acte music in B minor from *Rosamunde* was added. A year earlier the *Unfinished* Symphony had been published, one of the finest complete fragments of all time.

(In 1927 on the hundredth anniversary of Schubert's death a prize was offered for the completion of the *Unfinished* Symphony. It was as absurd as it would be to offer a prize for the restoration of the *Venus de Milo* at the Louvre. How had she held her arms that are lost? We have no desire to know. She is beautiful as she is.)

No Schubert scholar has been able to answer the one really pertinent question: Why did Schubert never mention the symphony and why did he leave it in two movements? The answer to this question is pure hypothesis. Perhaps Schubert left the symphony unfinished because he felt there was nothing more to be said. Why did Beethoven fail to write a third movement in his piano sonata Op. 111? Anton Schindler writes that the Master told him calmly (*gelassen*) that he had no time for a third movement, and thus had enlarged the second movement. But we know that Beethoven sketched and started a great many projects that were never completed. Schubert may not have been satisfied with the B minor Symphony and could not be bothered with it any more. That too is pure speculation. Brahms was more practical. He destroyed some works he was dissatisfied with, making life easier for his editors later on.

Modern scholars imply that Schubert may have been haunted by his B minor Symphony, that he may have had a sense of guilt for not finishing it, and therefore preferred not to see the score any more. That seems highly doubtful and inconsistent with what we know about Schubert. Creative artists occasionally leave some work unfinished and, instead of going back to it, start on something quite different. Did he want to banish the B minor Symphony from his consciousness and give it away, as has been suggested? Did he think that a two-movement symphony might never be performed and was therefore useless? That does not agree with his customary lack of concern about success or recognition. We know also that he refused to write certain things which some publishers asked him to write. He was Schubert and he always did as he pleased.

The two movements of the *Unfinished* Symphony have a similar time structure, three crotchets to the bar and three quavers to the bar, and are almost equal in length. But they are in different keys, a complete juxtaposition, as though Schubert had intended a daring and almost unique experiment. The miracle of the *Unfinished* Symphony is that it exists. It is an unpleasant thought that the servants of Anselm Hüttenbrenner might have used the manuscript to light another fire.

Schubert wrote music quickly. In no other way could he have produced in a relatively short time the enormous, though uneven output of musical works. On 5 September 1814, when he was seventeen, he inscribed at the end of the first movement of the String Quartet in B flat major, 'Written in four and a half hours.' It is a very good movement too. He was young and felt some pardonable boyish pride in his fast achievement.

Later he became more critical. He started work on a piano piece, was dissatisfied and so put it aside. He might go back to it later on. Instead of laboriously revising, as Beethoven did, Schubert would start on something completely different. His self-assurance was boundless; he knew he would never run out of musical ideas. When he was inspired he would get hold of the nearest piece of music paper and start writing. Once Anselm Hütten-brenner gave Schubert the original manuscript of Beethoven's song *Ich liebe dich*. It was a double sheet of music paper. Beethoven had written on the two outer pages, pages one and four. Schubert valued it highly but on one occasion he had a sudden idea and no other piece of paper to hand and thus used the two inner pages, pages two and three, to write a fast sketch of the Andante of his Piano Sonata in E flat major Op. 122. Underneath the sketch there is some scribbling as though he wanted to try out a new pen.

In 1820 Schubert wrote his famous *Quartettsatz* (String Quartet Movement) in C minor, another 'unfinished' work that is a short but complete masterpiece. Strict formalists have found fault with it – Einstein calls it 'not emotional but weird' – but it is full of Schubert's inspiration, full of singing melodies, the true expression of genius. Schubert intended to go on with it and he wrote an Andante in A flat major. But he did not finish it and put it away. The Andante remains a true fragment and was published as such in the Complete Edition.

In 1820 he also started work on a three-act operatic oratorio *Lazarus*. The full score of the first act and of half the second act exists. Various scenes from the New Testament are treated in an operatic manner. It is not certain whether Schubert completed it and the missing parts are lost, or whether it was another project he preferred to leave unfinished. *Lazarus* was publicly performed under Herbeck in 1863 in Vienna. Brahms wrote to his friend Joseph Joachim, the violinist, on 3 April, 'You may have read that here a *Lazarus* by Schubert had celebrated his resurrection after forty-three years. I have copied out several scenes . . . I could send them to you, and I promise you the greatest enjoyment.'

The mysterious fragment of the Scherzo that was to be the third movement of the *Unfinished* Symphony still exists. (The symphony would still be unfinished without a fourth movement, of which there is no trace.) The strange Scherzo consists of two pages of full score followed by a draft of a piano reduction. But after the first double bar the setting gets thinner. There is the beginning of the Trio, a waltz tune, but after sixteen bars the Trio suddenly ends. It is definitely unfinished. Could it be that Schubert lost his patience? Certainly not his musical imagination. He wrote many master-pieces in the six years that followed the *Unfinished* Symphony. He wrote the Great C major Symphony and perhaps he also wrote the so called Gmunden-Gastein Symphony that is lost (if it ever existed).

The widespread misunderstanding about the B minor Symphony, now called the *Unfinished* Symphony, is surpassed by the enigma of another symphony truly unfinished, on which Schubert worked in August 1821 – before he began writing the B minor. Only a slow introduction in E minor and 110 bars of the following Allegro in E major were written in full score. The rest of the four-movement symphony remains a genuine fragment, with a thin thread of melodies played by various instruments. There is also an occasional accompaniment. In 1846 Ferdinand Schubert gave this manu-script to Felix Mendelssohn as a token of his gratitude. Mendelssohn had done much for Schubert's Great C major Symphony in Leipzig.

Felix Mendelssohn died in 1847 and his brother Paul inherited the Schu-bert manuscript. In 1868 Paul Mendelssohn presented it in London to Sir George Grove, the noted Schubert scholar. Grove's enthusiasm for Schubert

Sir George Grove (*left*) and Sir Arthur Sullivan who in 1867 came to Vienna searching for Schubert manuscripts.

Brahms who took a
great interest in
Schubert's Unfinished
Symphony.

was not exactly a secret. In 1867 he and his friend Arthur Sullivan had gone
to Vienna searching for lost Schubert manuscripts. We know that they found
some missing parts of the *Rosamunde* music. Grove was delighted with Paul
Mendelssohn's present and immediately decided to give to the world 'a new
Schubert symphony'. He asked the English composer John Francis Barnett
to fill in the score of the E minor fragments.

Brahms was upset when he heard about this in Vienna. He wrote to Joseph
Joachim, who was in London, in December 1868:

I presume you know that Schubert's last symphony came by way of Ferdinand Schubert to Mendelssohn. The introduction and half the first movement are completed in full score. From then on the whole symphony is apparently sketched out, and in such a way that there are notes in every bar, a sight both lovely and sad, as I know from my own acquaintance with *Sakuntala* [an operatic sketch left by Schubert] ... This sketch [of the Schubert symphony] has long been thought lost. Now Paul Mendelssohn has sent it to London to Mr Grove! This would have seemed to me hard to believe, had I not read it in a letter from Mr Grove himself. If at all possible the symphony will now presumably be made usable post-haste for a performance.

Joseph Joachim.

Can you, or will you not try meanwhile to lay a restricting hand on it? ... If Mendelssohn did not have the courage to do it, and if you cannot find it either, then please make sure that no indecency is perpetrated with it!

Joachim could not, or would not, prevent John Francis Barnett from making Schubert's fragment 'usable post-haste for a performance'. It took place in London. Later a piano reduction of the score was published. In 1934 Felix von Weingartner published his version of the score with a great many errors. It is occasionally performed but Brahms' fears were justified. If Schubert had felt the urge to go on he would have written the symphony, he would not have left the fragment. There was plenty of time. Brahms was right: it was absolutely wrong to fill in the score.

It almost seems as though Schubert, who looked naïve and simple, left some complex problems about his symphonies – not to mention some smaller works – deliberately to prove that he was not simple at all. There is the *Unfinished* Symphony which we accept as one of his masterpieces, in two movements; there is the fragment, 'a sight both lovely and sad', of the so-called E minor symphony, which Brahms called mistakenly 'Schubert's last symphony' and which was later presented with a filled-in score; and there is the riddle of the Gastein or Gmunden-Gastein symphony which seems to exist only in the letters of Schubert's friends.

In 1864 Spaun wrote in his reminiscences, 'In Gastein he (Schubert) composed his greatest and most beautiful symphony.' Schubert was in Gastein in the summer of 1825. Leopold Sonnleithner, usually a reliable source, writes, 'Schubert composed uninvited his Great Symphony for the (Philharmonic) Music Society to whom he presented the autograph.' The presentation happened on 9 October 1826. Among the witnesses were Bauernfeld, Schober, Sonnleithner, Spaun, and Ferdinand Schubert.

But the manuscript of the Great C major Symphony is dated by Schubert himself March 1828. Schubert usually put the date down when he began working on a piece. This raises several questions that have kept the Schubert scholars busy and arguing to this day: is the Great Symphony which Schubert presented to the Music Society in 1826 identical with the Great C major, dated March 1828?; did Schubert work on it in Gastein in 1825?; or was there a Gastein or Gmunden-Gastein symphony, of which every trace is lost?

As usual the experts are no help. K.F. Pohl, Librarian and Historian of the Music Society at the time of the presentation, claimed that the work of 1825 and the Great C major Symphony were identical. No separate Gastein symphony existed. But O.E. Deutsch states clearly, 'Pohl was wrong in supposing that the Great C major was written in 1826 and only revised in 1828.' Maurice J. E. Brown speaks of the possibility that the earlier symphony and the C major might be the same but reaches no definite conclusion. Hans Gal has no doubts. '1828 was again a year of colossal productivity. Its harvest was the Great C major Symphony.' The British scholar John Reed writes, 'Pohl was clearly right in concluding that the manuscript of the Great C major is the manuscript which Schubert scored in 1826 and presented to the Music Society, which the Society failed to perform, and which Schubert revised and dated with a view to publication in March 1828.' Even then the Great C major was neither performed nor published.

Reed rejects the possibility of a mysterious, lost Gastein symphony. And he asks a sensible question: 'Does it matter whether the Great C major Symphony was written in 1825 or 1828?' Not to musicians and not to the public. But it certainly matters to Reed. 'The answer can only be that nothing can matter more to our idea of Schubert's development, indeed that no consistent account can be given, until the question is resolved.' Will the question ever be resolved?

Postscript

Schubert's Great C major Symphony, which he finished in the summer of 1828, a few months before his death, was not performed in his lifetime. For ten years after the composer's death no one looked for it. In the autumn of 1838 Robert Schumann came to Vienna on a musical pilgrimage. Like other composers he was aware of the *genius loci*. He visited the graves of the great composers. He spent a long time at the grave of Schubert and later went to see Schubert's brother Ferdinand. They talked about Franz and Schumann returned several times. At that time Ferdinand spoke of himself as Schubert's sole heir. He kept his brother's manuscripts in a black polished chest. There Schumann discovered the Great C major Symphony.

'Finally Ferdinand had allowed me to see some of Franz Schubert's compositions. The riches that lay here piled up made me tremble with pleasure. Where to begin, where to stop?' And then the excitement when Schumann discovered the great symphony that had been overlooked. He was overcome:

Who knows how long it would have lain neglected there in dust and darkness, had I not immediately arranged with Ferdinand Schubert to send it to the management of the Gewandhams Concerts in Leipzig, to the artist himself who conducts them (Felix Mendelssohn) . . . The symphony reached Leipzig where it was performed, its greatness recognized, performed again and received with delighted and almost universal admiration. The enterprising firm of Breitkopf & Härtel bought the work and the copyright, and thus the orchestral parts are now available to us, soon perhaps to be followed by the full score, for the benefit and enjoyment of the whole world. . . .

Schumann was elated but the score was published only ten years later. The 'almost universal admiration' was limited first to Leipzig. It was remembered that Schubert had offered the C major Symphony to the Vienna Philharmonic Society. They declined it because it was 'too long and too difficult'. Schumann himself commented on the 'heavenly length' of the symphony's last movement. 'How refreshing is this feeling of overflowing wealth! With others we always tremble for the conclusion and we are troubled lest we find ourselves disappointed.'

opposite The score of the Great C major symphony.

211

Schubert's 'heavenly length' is now understood as the composer's enthusiasm, his wealth of ideas, his romantic inability to contain his exuberance, as Schumann so well knew. It is not, as some people now assume, the lack of imagination that made him stretch out his ideas. Even when Schubert is 'heavenly' for a long time, he is never a bore.

Mendelssohn loved the symphony and conducted it twice after the first performance on 21 March 1839. The Vienna Philharmonic performed the first two movements on 15 December, inserting in between an aria from Donizetti's *Lucia di Lammermoor*. The critic of Castelli's *Allgemeiner musikalischer Anzeiger* wrote:

The two movements of the symphony certainly left no one in doubt as to the composer's thorough grounding in the art of composition. But Schubert seemed to be unable fully to succeed with the tonal masses. The result was a kind of skirmish of instruments out of which no effectual pattern emerged. True, a red thread ran through the whole but it was too pink for one to detect it correctly. In my opinion it would have been better to have left the work strictly alone.

Not only the publishers but the music critics too showed a sad lack of understanding for Schubert's art. The critic neglected to explain how he detected 'a thread running through the whole' since he had heard only the first two movements of the symphony. Yet he was lucky. In Paris in 1844 Habeneck's Orchestra, after a rehearsal, refused to go beyond the first movement.

Schumann was among the few who truly understood the great symphony. 'Deep down in this work there lies more than mere song, more than mere joy and sorrow, as already expressed in music in a hundred other instances. It transports us into a world where I cannot recall ever having been before.'

The twelfth-century minnesinger, Walther von der Vogelweide, sang of Austria 'where I learned to sing and compose ... *am wünniclichen Hof ze Wiene* (at the wonderful Court of Vienna)'. Ever since musicians have learned to sing and compose in Vienna. The city's musical mood and its stimulating effect were known for centuries. No one was ever able to rationally explain it. It may be a mixture of traditions and echoes, of the melodious Viennese landscape, of the songs of the peoples who came through the valley of the Danube. Vienna's *genius loci* is an accepted fact, not a legend. It attracted musicians and composers throughout the centuries and made Vienna the birthplace of various schools of Western music.

Many houses, streets, squares in Vienna remain associated with music. There is Beethoven Weg, a path leading up toward Kahlenberg where Beethoven loved to walk. To Schindler, Beethoven said, 'Here I composed *Szene*

am Bach.' 'Scene by the Brook' is from the *Pastoral* Symphony whose movements are prefaced by Beethoven's own inscriptions, such as 'Cheerful
impressions received on arriving in the country'.

Inexplicably the great composers were often misunderstood in Vienna.
If they were lucky they were talked about and maligned. The unlucky ones,
like Schubert, were simply ignored. The Viennese have shown a persistent
lack of understanding for genius. In 1878 Brahms wrote, 'That people in
general do not understand and do not respect the greatest things, such as
Mozart's concertos, helps our kind to live and require renown.' Brahms first
came to Vienna in 1862, though he did not expect to stay there. He hoped
to become director of the Philharmonic Concerts in his native Hamburg.
'I live here ten steps from the Prater and can drink my wine where Beethoven
drank his.' Joseph Hellmesberger told him, 'You are the heir of Beethoven.'
On 16 November, after he performed his Piano Quartet in A major Op.
26 with the Hellmesberger Quartet, he wrote to his parents that 'the Viennese public stimulates me more than ours (in Hamburg)'. Later he was less
enthusiastic about many Viennese who became partisans of Bruckner and
had no use for Brahms. He once said, 'Are Bruckner's works immortal or
perhaps even symphonies? Don't make me laugh.'

On his first visit Brahms stayed several months. He visited 'the sanctified
places' where his predecessors had lived and worked. He was exhilarated
'to be treading on classical soil'. He began to read some of Schubert's unpublished manuscripts and tried to get them accepted by his publisher
Rieter-Biedermann in Switzerland.

My best hours here I owe to the unprinted works of Schubert of which I have quite
a number at home in manuscript. Yet however delightful and enjoyable it is to con-
template them, everything else about this music is sad. I have many things here
in manuscript belonging to [the publisher] Spina or to [Schubert's nephew]
Schneider of which nothing exists but just the manuscript, not a single copy. And
neither at Spina's nor with me are they kept in fireproof cabinets. . . .

After much hesitation Rieter-Biedermann published some of Schubert's
works, among them the Mass in E flat major. Brahms scored several Schubert
songs for Julius Stockhausen, including *Im Abendrot* and *Der Einsame*, after
two poems by Carl Lappe from Pommerania. Five years earlier Stockhausen
had sung Schubert's *Die schöne Müllerin* as a complete cycle in Vienna. He
had earned three times more than Schubert had originally received for his
Lieder. Musical life in Vienna was getting commercial. That prominent performers earn much more money than the composers whose works they perform is a sad, old story. In 1861 Stockhausen had sung the cycle in Hamburg,
with Brahms at the piano. Later Stockhausen sang Schubert's songs all over

Europe. In St Petersburg he was accompanied by Anton Rubinstein. Stockhausen was said to have a small but expressive baritone voice, very suitable for Schubert's *Lieder*.

Stockhausen took the manuscripts of the Schubert songs that Brahms had scored for him to England. There they later disappeared. In 1863 Stockhausen was appointed Director of the Philharmonic Concerts in Hamburg. It was the position Brahms had hoped for and he was disappointed. Joseph Joachim angrily wrote that 'the affront to Johannes will be remembered by history'. Brahms found some consolation when Vienna's Singakademie, the choir of the Gesellschaft der Musikfreunde, appointed him as choir master. It was a job that carried a great deal of prestige. By that time Schubert was famous.

In 1843 Heinrich Heine reported in *Lutetia* that Paris was inundated with songs by 'an unidentified Monsieur Schubert'. In 1862 Eduard Hanslick wrote in Vienna, 'Schubert had been dead for over thirty years and yet it is as though he continued to work invisibly. One can hardly keep up with him.' Between 1881 and 1883 Dr Eduard Schneider, the nephew of Schubert, sold many Schubert manuscripts to Nikolaus Dumba for 6000 florins. Dumba, one of the new Ringstrasse financiers and millionaires, loved the arts and spent much money on artists. Once he sent Hans Makart, the painter, to Venice at his expense. Makart returned with flamboyant ideas and later painted the frieze in the ceremonial dining room of Dumba's palais. Dumba was well acquainted with Katharina Schratt, the Burgtheater actress and great friend of Emperor Franz Joseph I. Dumba was a prominent Ringstrasse Maecenas. Had Schubert been alive he would have made him his protégé. After Dumba's death in 1900 his collection of Schubert manuscripts was divided. The symphonies, except No. 5 and the last, went to the Gesellschaft der Musikfreunde. All other remaining manuscripts were bequeathed to the Vienna Stadtbibliothek, the City Library.

The first Complete Edition of Franz Schubert's works was arranged by Breitkopf & Härtel between 1884 and 1897. They were probably trying to forget how the predecessors in the firm had treated Schubert while he was alive. Schubert's *Lieder* were edited and revised by Eusebius Mandyczewski, the prominent Viennese musicologist who showed great care and reverence in his work. Mandyczewski used, above all, Schubert's autographs whenever possible and original editions with opus numbers marked by Schubert. He also included the oldest available editions of the *Lieder* that had not been published while Schubert was alive, as well as copies made by Schubert's friends, Albert Stadler and Josef Wilhelm Witteczek. Stadler had begun as early as 1815 to copy every song written by his Stadtkonvikt classmate Schubert. That was often difficult because Schubert's manuscripts would mysteriously disappear among his many friends, but eventually Stadler had three volumes of copies. Witteczek copied and collected later on. They were not interested in autographs which were considered of no special value until Aloys Fuchs began collecting them. A great many of Schubert's original manuscripts have disappeared. Without the enthusiasm of Stadler and Witteczek many Schubert *Lieder* might have been lost.

Towards the end of the century the impact of Schubert's work began to be felt. In 1883 Gustav Mahler worked on his *Lieder eines fahrenden Gesellen*. In the last *Lied*, the melody 'Auf der Strasse steht ein Lindenbaum' is consciously shaped after Schubert's *Der Lindenbaum*.

Around the turn of the century the inevitable happened: Schubert was 'discovered' by commercially minded playwrights, librettists, novelists, and musical arrangers. Suddenly everybody saw a goldmine in Franz Schubert, the jolly Biedermeier character. Johann Raudnitz wrote a one-act play *Horch, horch, die Lerch!* in which Schubert was shown 'between two women he loves', Therese Grob and Caroline Esterházy. No comment is needed. Karl Costa wrote a *Volksstück, Franz Schubert*; he too took bizarre liberties with the composer's biography. The most popular effort of this kind, the operetta *Das Dreimäderlhaus*, known as *Blossom Time* or *Lilac Time*, has done more to distort and spread the phoney Schubert legend than anything else. And then came the various films about Schubert. Any similarity to Schubert's life and work was purely accidental.

Today people want to know all there is to know about Schubert; they want to know the truth. Above all the truth is in his music. Almost Schubert's entire output has been critically edited in the Complete Editions. New sources are still found and former errors are eliminated. There is also a tendency to rediscover some 'forgotten' masterpiece, often for doubtful reasons. Performers are certain of much publicity when they perform a work that has never been heard, even if it turns out to be a second-class work.

As a rule a composer's most famous works are also his best. The famous string quartets by Haydn and Mozart are better than the less famous ones. Beethoven's Fifth Symphony is universally admired as the great classical symphony. Taste is a subjective, often elusive, phenomenon. Verdi's late masterpieces *Otello* and *Falstaff* are greater works of art than his earlier works *Rigoletto* and *La Traviata*, which however remain more popular.

In the case of Schubert most of his early symphonies, early string quartets, overtures and rondos do not reach the greatness of the last string quartets, the String Quintet, the *Unfinished* Symphony and the Great C major Symphony. Again there is an exception, his *Lieder*. He was only seventeen when he wrote *Gretchen am Spinnrade*. It is incredible but true. Genius knows no age, no rules. Schubert's immortality as an instrumental composer rests on about a dozen masterpieces of piano, chamber music and orchestra. Some of his choral and sacred music could be added to that list but not his operas.

Fortunately musical popularization is no longer fashionable. Since the days of Mahler, Toscanini and George Szell musicians everywhere go back to the original sources, whenever possible. 'Toscanini wiped out the arbitrariness of the post-romantic interpreters,' Szell once said. 'He did away with the meretricious tricks and the thick incrustation of interpretative nuances that had been piling up for decades.'

Szell defined classical music – which in its fullest sense includes Schubert – as music in which 'precise enunciation and articulation of every note, every nuance, every phrase matters a great deal, because classical music should have no colouristic frills. Every phrase must be so carefully shaped that its sense will be perceived by the listener as clearly as the sense of a line by Shakespeare.'

All composers depend on how their music is interpreted and re-created. In this respect Schubert, the composer of *Lieder*, is at a disadvantage. The human voice is the most difficult musical instrument of all. Schubert himself seems to have sung reasonably well but he might be quite pleased to hear his *Lieder* sung by some of the leading interpreters today. The art of *Lieder* singing has reached a very high level, owing to the technical perfection demanded by the latest recordings. Schubert would not be surprised though. He certainly heard his songs in his inner ear when he wrote them; he knew instinctively how they should sound.

Great singers have written about the problems and difficulties of performing Schubert's *Lieder*. There are important nuances, almost inaudible accents, vowels to be pronounced and consonants that must be articulated. It is insufficient to sing a Schubert *Lied* technically well. It must be musically and spiritually understood. The phrases must be shaped meaningfully; as Szell said, 'every phrase matters a great deal.' And there is the music between and behind the notes, the inner content which even precise musical notation cannot convey. Every time a singer performs a Schubert *Lied* he re-creates a part of Schubert. The best interpreters always understood that. Lotte Lehmann, the only woman who recorded *Die schöne Müllerin*, in her book *More Than Singing* gave her personal feelings and solid practical advice on how to sing these songs. About *Thränenregen* she writes,

... You lean down toward the brook and see its waters, like a luminous veil, rippling on over the image of your beloved ... Sing mysteriously, calling and yet listening

... Lift out the two words 'Geselle, Geselle' like a call, sing them separated from the continuing musical phrase.

Noted pianists have also written about the cycle. Gerald Moore who recorded *Die schöne Müllerin* several times, thrice with Fischer-Dieskau, says about *Thränenregen*,

... Once again our Schubert comes up with a telling stroke in the final bars. Hope and despair are in those four bars. ... The pianist allows us to hear this dramatic change by a distinct hesitation before the minor chord, as if reluctant to accept the inevitable.

Such advice, in connection with the artists' recordings, helps us to understand the complexities of Schubert. Among the finest interpreters of the cycle were Peter Pears and Benjamin Britten. It has been said that when Britten played Schubert he had almost become Schubert. 'The imagery of the final *Müllerin* songs is the recurrent imagery of Britten's own œuvre . . . (Schubert's stream) lives in the piano part. I have still to hear it played on such a piano as Schubert himself knew, light, silvery, and clear; Britten comes closest to making a modern concert grand sound right.' (Andrew Porter)

A whole book of analysis could be written about Schubert's influence on later composers many of whom were not even aware that the unending stream of Schubert's melodies had flowed into their musical consciousness. The more one knows about Schubert the greater he gets.

It is a formidable task to stand up and sing these often deceptively simple songs. Sometimes they are the hardest to perform. Schubert was not thinking of public performances when he wrote his earlier songs. Song recitals were unknown. He wrote the songs because he felt compelled to write them and he hoped his friends, and their friends, would like them. Only late in his life did he think of professional artists when he wrote his *Lieder* and the cycles. Sometimes the vocal range does not exceed more than a ninth, and they can be sung by amateurs, by anybody with a voice. But one thing all his *Lieder* have in common: they are an intimate art form. They express a very personal feeling and spiritual meaning. Ideally they should be sung exactly as he wrote them. He permitted himself and his interpreters no drastic liberties, but he was explicit about singer and pianist being one and about expressing the inner meaning of a *Lied*.

The art of Schubert remains synonymous with melody. From his earliest efforts as a composer to his last fourteen songs, *Schwanengesang*, Schubert was surrounded by melodies. His greatest melodies are essentially simple, following the melodic lines of Haydn and Mozart. He was enormously gifted and his teachers soon realized that there was little he did not instinctively know. Wenzel Ruzitska who was Schubert's harmony teacher at the Stadtkonvikt would say of his pupil, 'He has learnt it all from God.' Some able composers – Schumann, Brahms, Richard Strauss – studied Schubert's 'simple' melodies, trying hard to create some that sounded similar and failed.

In 1918 Richard Strauss said to Max Marschalk:

The most perfect melodic shapes are found in Mozart. He has the lightness of touch which is the true objective. With Beethoven the melodies are heavier; one is clearly conscious of the labour. Listen to the remarkable expansion of a Mozart melody, to Cherubino's 'Voi, che sapete' for instance. You think it is coming to an end, but it goes ever further.

Strauss wrote operas and his lifelong idol was Mozart. But Mozart himself would have admired Schubert's melodic inventiveness. Schubert often woke up in the morning with a wonderful tune in his head. It could truly be said of him that the gods had given him the melody while he was asleep. Schubert's melodies are fundamentally different from the melodies of the Italians. He did not impress Wagner and Verdi hardly knew him.

Yet today, when the world gets noisier all the time and loudness is often mistaken for beauty of sound, Schubert's melodies – simple and innocent – seem the most modern of all. They affect us because they are so natural. Each of us could have thought of them if . . . we like to think. None of us would have thought of a Bellini melody or a Mozart melody. But the simple and incredibly beautiful melody that forms the second subject in the first movement of the *Unfinished* Symphony seems to come from the heart, as Beethoven said in another connection, and goes straight to the heart. Yet musicians know that this simple, natural melody is constructed by a great master. And Schubert's so called folk songs, such as *Der Lindenbaum*, have the subtle development of great art songs but are so well done that we do not notice how much art went into them. It is this seeming simplicity that gives Schubert's melodies their eternal value. They will be sung as long as people want to sing.

Around the turn of the century Vienna's Schubertbund began to perform many works of Schubert that had been unknown. Then came Professor Otto Erich Deutsch who laboriously and accurately proved that the sober truth about Schubert was often less colourful than the romantic legend. In 1936 Deutsch discovered the scores of *Geheimes*, *An Schwager Kronos* and *Memnon* in the library of Windsor Castle and had them published, also Brahms' choral version with orchestra of *Gruppe aus dem Tartarus*. Brahms once said that among the hundreds of Schubert's *Lieder* there was not one 'from which one

couldn't learn something'. In 1948 Deutsch published in London his Thematic Catalogue of Schubert's Works. A German edition is now being prepared. In 1939 Deutsch went to Cambridge, England, to continue his life's
work. He died in 1967. 'The Schubert research lost its most outstanding
pioneer,' wrote Fischer-Dieskau. But Deutsch remains unforgotten. Musicians referring to the works of Schubert are now using the more complete
D (Deutsch) numbers instead of the old opus numbers, just as they use K
(Köchel) numbers when thinking of the work of Mozart.

In 1964 the American Musical Society, in co-operation with the Musical
Library Association, reprinted the Breitkopf & Härtel Edition of Schubert's
Collected Works. Since 1969 the Bärenreiter-Verlag in Kassel, Germany,
has been publishing a new complete edition of the works of Schubert; so
far twelve volumes of the new edition have been brought out. Schubert's
Lieder are edited by Walther Dürr, Arnold Feil and Christa Landon. New
sources have been found and some discoveries have been made. Schubert
autographs and copies of unpublished works were discovered in the archive
of Vienna's Männergesangs-Verein. Among them were the songs *Vollendung*
and *Die Erde* that were long believed to be lost.

Unlike Mandyczewski who listed Schubert's *Lieder* chronologically in the
earlier Breitkopf & Härtel edition, the editors of the new edition arranged
the songs in several groups. First they put together the *Lieder* that were
published while Schubert was alive and which he grouped himself. For the
songs – most of them – which Schubert never saw published the editors follow
the Thematic Catalogue by Deutsch. When Schubert set the same poem
to music twice or several times the earliest version is logically seen as the
beginning of the group. Whenever possible the editors follow Schubert's own
selections, which creates an intimate connection between the songs. They
also try to re-create Schubert's original notation as closely as possible. The
new piano accompaniment is often different, closer to Schubert, than the
earlier publications. The new edition re-creates the art of Schubert more
faithfully than the former one.

It is an enormous job and will take a long time. Few great composers
have suffered so much editing, arranging, improving and plain distortion
in the past one hundred and fifty years. Yet if any composer deserves to
be understood in simple human terms and to be resurrected in his heroic
greatness it is Franz Schubert.

Select Bibliography

Complete Edition of Schubert's Works, Editors' Report (E. Mandyczewski, J.N. Fuchs, J. Brüll, J. Epstein)

O.E. Deutsch, *Schubert, Documents of His Life and Work* (London, 1946)

O.E. Deutsch, *Schubert: Complete Thematic Catalogue of His Works* (London, 1951)

O.E. Deutsch, *Schubert, Memoirs by His Friends* (London, 1958)

O.E. Deutsch, *Franz Schubert, Briefe und Schriften* (Vienna, 1954)

M.G.E. Brown, *Franz Schubert, A Critical Biography* (London, 1958)

Richard Capell, *Schubert's Songs* (London, 1928)

Alfred Einstein, *Schubert* (New York, 1951)

John Reed, *Schubert, The Final Years* (London, 1972)

Dietrich Fischer-Dieskau, *Auf den Spuren der Schubert-Lieder* (Wiesbaden, 1974)

Hans Gal, *Franz Schubert and The Essence of Melody* (London, 1974)

Harry Goldschmidt, *Franz Schubert, Ein Lebensbild* (Berlin, 1954)

Heinrich Kreissle von Hellborn, *Franz Schubert* (Vienna, 1865)

Paul Stefan, *Franz Schubert* (Vienna, 1928)

Paul Mies, *Schubert, der Meister des Liedes* (Berne, 1928)

Paul Henry Lang, *Music In Western Civilization* (New York, 1941)

Acknowledgments

Photographs were supplied or are reproduced by kind permission of the following:

Bavaria Verlag: 20, *32 (top and bottom)*, 38 (left) (Direktion der Museen der Stadt Wien), 42, 45 (top), 47, 48 (top right)*, 51, 56*, 123 (Direktion der Museen der Stadt Wien), 125, 126 (Direktion der Museen der Stadt Wien), 146*, 152 (bottom), 153, 164–5, 167, 168–9, 170, 173, *185, 186, 187.*

Bildarchiv der Österreichische Nationalbibliothek: 15*, 27, 36 (bottom)*, 38 (right), 48 (top left)*, 48 (bottom), 50 (bottom), 53*, 59, 62, 64–5, 67, 68 (right and left), 72–3, 74*, 77, 78, 79*, 86, 87 (top and bottom), 97*, 108*, 118, 121*, 122*, 129*, 130*, 144*, 147*, 148 (right and left), 151 (left and right), 162, 172, 176*, 182, 192.

Photographie Bulloz: 11, 12.

Mary Evans Picture Library: 49.

Fotomas Index: 24 (bottom), 26.

Gesellschaft der Musikfreunde in Wien: 19, 45 (bottom), 75, *81*, 98, 100–101, 104, *133*, 196, 199.

Heeresgeschichtlichen Museum, Vienna: *30–1*.

By gracious permission of Her Majesty the Queen: 33.

Historisches Museum der Stadt Wien: *29 (top and bottom)*, *81, 82, 134–5, 136, 188.*

Kester Lichtbild-Archiv: 205.

The Mansell Collection: 36 (top), 57, 94, 152 (top), 179, 193, 203 (left and right), 204.

München, Neue Pinakothek: *84*.

Radio Times Hulton Picture Library: 24 (top), 34, 50 (top), 71, 80, 99, 103, 107, 113, 180.

Ullstein Bilderdienst: 35, 69, 70, 158, 190.

Weidenfeld and Nicolson Archive: 16, 28, 91.

* From the Historisches Museum der Stadt Wien.

Numbers in italics indicate colour photographs.

Index